BRITISH
WARSHIPS
...ES

GW00507571

HMS Duncan

THE ROYAL NAVY

National defence should be the first priority of any government. Putting in place the infrastructure, equipment and personnel to ensure the safety of country, citizens and interests, both domestic and overseas is a duty that should be at the forefront of any political leaders agenda. To this end successive governments have formulated various defence manifestos in the form of Defence Reviews - setting out policy, strategic ambition and shaping the armed forces to achieve those aims. Some Defence Reviews are well thought out - others nothing more than a vehicle for cutting expenditure. The failure of the system is that, most governments just get one opportunity per term for implementing defence policy and by the time the next government assumes the mantle of power, the whole review process starts again.

The Strategic Defence and Security Review set out by the Conservative led coalition in 2010, was ill-thought out and aimed to reshape the forces to counter the perceived threats from 2020. This vision of Future Force 2020 may indeed turn out to be adequate for the job in hand in 17 years time, but unfortunately the SDSR was accompanied by the savage slashing of current equipment, creating massive capability gaps, in the misguided belief that nothing untoward would happen during the transition from the Armed Forces of 2010, to those slimmed down capabilities required in 2020. However, within months the government were caught off-guard by the unforseen events of the "Arab Spring". Suddenly there was a requirement for capabilities which had already been withdrawn, gapped and scrapped. Some of the units used in the subsequent combat and relief operations had their withdrawal temporarily suspended while they provided vital support to deployed operations. This whole series of events proved how quickly world events can change and how ludicrous it is to try and shape Armed Forces for a percivale threat so far in the future, while at the same time gambling with capability gaps in the hope that nothing would crop up in the interim. There will be another review in 2015 under the new guidelines set out by the government, but already, only halfway down that road, the whole process has been shown to be flawed. Although it is seeded with grandiose ideas of shaping a modern efficient fighting force capable of projecting power around the globe and flexible enough to deploy rapidly and in strength, the facts have shown themselves to be nothing more than another ploy to save millions of pounds by cutting much needed capability today with the promise that by 2020, miraculously, the UK Armed Forces will be properly trained, equipped and supported to carry out the will of the government - one might suggest that in order for that to happen, the current coalition need to significantly decrease their global ambitions to match the reduced forces they are prepared to fund.

As recently as November 2012, in a speech to the Oxford University department of politics and international relations, the Chief of the Defence Staff warned that defence cuts have left him unable to carry out everything the Government demands. General Sir David Richards said ministers' demands had not been revised to correspond with the reduced size of the Armed Forces. He also expressed concern over the ability of the RN to carry out its tasks with so few frigates and destroyers saying that he found it troubling that £1 billion destroyers were deployed on anti-piracy operations to combat dhows armed with RPGs.

With Future Force 2020 still a long way off the Royal Navy continues to operate in places as distant as the Caribbean in the west to the Gulf and South China Sea in the east; the North Atlantic to the Falkland Islands and Antarctica to the south, with ever decreasing assets. The next review is just two years away. With the economy still trying to recover and public spending still being squeezed, what hope is there that the RN won't, once again, find itself being cut in an effort to further reduce the defence budget.

Under the SDSR the coalition determined that the future aircraft carriers should be capable of operating the F-35C conventional carrier variant of the Joint Strike Fighter and that the ships should have catapults and arrester gear to accommodate such operations. They called it "lunacy to order 65,000 ton carriers without 'cats and traps'". SDSR looked hard at the issue of interoperablility and determined that the F-35B would not be fully interoperable with key allies, since their jets would not be able to land on them. *"Pursuit of closer partnership is a core strategic principle for the SDSR because it is clear that the UK will, in most circumstances, act militarily as part of a wider coalition. We will therefore install catapult and arrester gear".*

This support for a full carrier strike capability came at a price. With no immediate need for a carrier strike capability it was determined that ARK ROYAL and the full complement of Harrier aircraft were to be decommissioned with immediate effect, thereby gapping carrier strike until 2020 at the earliest, but the coalition were convinced that it was a capability loss for which they could mitigate through the use of RAF assets. Less than a year later this was put to the test during the Arab Spring and combat operations over Libya. RAF strike aircraft had to forward deploy to land bases in Italy and Cyprus. Their logistics supply chain saw massive road convoys stretching the length of Europe as they strove to keep a handful of aircraft equipped, serviced, fuelled and armed. France, Italy and the USA simple deployed aircraft carriers and assault ships off the coast of Libya from where they were able to launch reactive and timely strikes without the need for basing rights to foreign airfields, long transit flights and the need for air-to-air refuelling at huge cost.

Although the government continued to insist that the carrier strike capability was neither missed nor required for the Libya operation, they very soon performed a complete U-turn and determined that the correct way ahead for the UK carriers was to abandon 'cat and trap' and revert to the original ski-jumps and the F-35B vertical take-off and landing (VSTOL) variant of the aircraft, citing that, one, they were no longer prepared to wait until 2020 to fill the carrier strike gap, two, that the F-35B was further developed than the F-35C and three, that converting a single carrier would cost close to £2 billion. Without further fanfare that was that.

The crass stupidity of this volte-face, just to save cash in the short term, over a programme that will see these ships in service for the next fifty years, defies belief. Why was it so expensive to install cat and trap when the ships were designed to receive such a fit as and when it was deemed relevant. Indeed, the French version of the very same ship was designed from the outset to use conventional aircraft. What we are now faced with is a ship that can only operate VSTOL fixed wing aircraft, thereby being of no use to a coalition task force as French, and US aircraft will not be able to operate from their decks. Secondly, it denies the UK the ability of deploying a fully integrated air wing which would include airborne early warning and electronic warfare aircraft. The public (and ministers it would seem) believe that stealth characteristics mean that an aircraft can penetrate enemy airspace and deliver its ordnance without the need for support. This is very wrong. Stealth aircraft come in behind Airrorne Early Warning aircraft (AWACS) which monitor the airspace and Electronic Warfare aircraft (EW) which jam and supress air defences, creating a sanitised area for the stealth aircraft to operate. The only stealth aircraft shot down in combat was an F-117 lost during the Balkans war - it was lost because they flew despite the EW aircraft being unavailable.

Projecting forward across the life of the ships, who will be developing the next generation of VSTOL aircraft or is it anticipated that we will still operate the elderly F-35B in 2070? The future is likely to be unmanned air vehicles, but the truth is that most of these would also require cat and trap.

We also have to look at how viable the F-35 programme is. Even now the UK does not know how much an F-35B will cost. There was a requirement for 150 aircraft, but we will now only get as many as our budget will allow and who knows how few that will be.

We then have to look at the continuation of the programme into the future. Much has been said about its spiralling costs and continuing technical problems. There was much debate in the US as to how survivable this programme will be in future budget negotiations. Perhaps with the US election now settled there will be some progress with US defence budgets. However, there are then issues with

4

supporting the aircraft at sea. The US Navy is having serious concerns about the logistics of operating this aircraft from a carrier. Spare engines are too big to fit in the current generation of transport aircraft; the stealth coatings require specialist application and some maintenance issues would require the aircraft being returned to the factory - all of this is in addition to ongoing technical issues with aircraft systems and sensors.

The good news is that the carrier programme is forging a head, with most of the hull of QUEEN ELIZABETH assembled. The bad news however, is that constant dithering by the government in order to achieve short term savings will now deny the RN the ability to deploy a fully integrated strike carrier capability. The government will argue that the RN will have a carrier strike capability but realistically the RNs super carriers will have to operate on the periphery of any future strike operations being able to offer just a handful of very expensive, very short range strike aircraft and none of the associated support aircraft required for a strike package. On the bright side, the RAF seem not to have a use for a VSTOL aircraft so perhaps the RN will once again be in charge of its own fixed wing aircraft.

The government is also forging ahead with the Successor submarine programme - the replacement for the Trident missile carrying Vanguard class submarines. At the same time the Liberal Democrat side of the coalition are reviewing alternative options for providing the deterrent, ranging from having the ability to deploy weapons, but keeping the missiles in store through to using short range nuclear-tipped cruise missiles. Again the government are getting themselves in a mess over definitions of military capability. A deterrent can only be effective if it has a 24 hours a day, seven days a week, 365 days a year capability. That is why the imperative is for a continuous at sea deterrent. Any enemy knows that if it were to launch a strike, there would be immediate retaliation. It is that immediacy that deters potential aggressors. Any other option is merely a nuclear strike capability. So is the UK to have a nuclear deterrent or a nuclear strike capability - two totally different things.

This year will see the end of the destroyer replacement programme. The final Type 45, DUNCAN, will be delivered and the last of the elderly Type 42s, EDINBURGH, will be decommissioned. A programme that was originally to have delivered twelve ships on a one for one replacement basis has in fact delivered just half that number. The worry now is that as the frigate replacement programme, the Type 26, begins to take shape, there is already talk of a 'like for like' replacement with the thirteen Type 23s in service. As has already been mentioned the RN destroyer/frigate force is operating at maximum tempo with just 19 ships (rather than the 32 deemed a minium just a few years ago). If the Type 23 programme goes along the same lines as the earlier Type 45 we can standby for a reduction in numbers with the government rolling out its oft used argument that 'improved capability means that we can do the same tasking with fewer hulls'. I hope that I am proved wrong.

In recent months there have been calls from Portsmouth MPs for the RN to order more Offshore Patrol Vessels in an effort to keep shipbuilding alive at Portsmouth once the carrier work is complete - the MoD however claim that there is no requirement for further OPVs at the present.

At present the RN operates just four OPVs (three River class with the Fishery Protection Squadron and CLYDE, permanently based in the Falkland Islands). In recent months however, with the maritime patrol aircraft being consigned to the scrapheap, the only way of monitoring our offshore waters, installations and fisheries is with an increased OPV fleet. Recently UK fishing boats were surrounded and attacked by their French counterparts in international waters off the French coast over what has been termed the Scallop Wars - there was no OPV to police the incident and of course no MPA to provide reconnaissance. Spain has, in recent months, become even more belligerent over the Bay of Gibraltar - regularly entering British Gibraltar Territorial Waters with Guardia Civile patrol craft and more recently Spanish Navy Patrol Frigates. The days of a Gibraltar Guardship are long past, and the Gibraltar Squadron do what they can with the tiny SCIMITAR and SABRE and a handful of RiBs, but unless the UK deploy a more robust patrolling capability, these incursions and incidents from a NATO partner will continue unchecked. With the limited number of destroyers and frigates in the fleet and the increasing demand for RN warships to deploy on operations, such as anti-piracy and counter-drugs, which can be considered more of a constabulary, is it not time to look at the balance between high end warships and OPVs - it does not make sense to deploy limited, and sophisticated, air defence assets such as the Type 45 destroyers, to conduct policing duties that could just a easily be carried out by smaller corvette sized vessels. The Omani Khaleef class, built in the UK and based on the River class would seem ideal. Reasonably armed and with a good turn of speed and capable of embarking a Lynx-type helicopter it would only cost around £100 million per ship.

In two years time there will be another defence review. In that time the MoD need to seriously address how the RN is to operate in Future Force 2000 because on current progress and with current budgets, important programmes such as the aircraft carriers, nuclear deterrent and frigate/destroyer force are not going to be able to deliver the capability the government is advocating. Although the RN will never admit it, they are going to continue to be stretched and as a result be less able to commit the correct type of ship, in sufficient numbers to meet the ever increasing demands and tasking placed on them.

Steve Bush
Plymouth, December 2012

SHIPS OF THE ROYAL NAVY
Pennant Numbers

Ship	Pennant Number	Page	Ship	Pennant Number	Page
Helicopter Carriers			**Submarines**		
ILLUSTRIOUS	R06	13	VANGUARD	S28	9
			VICTORIOUS	S29	9
Assault Ships			VIGILANT	S30	9
			VENGEANCE	S31	9
OCEAN	L12	14	TIRELESS	S88	12
ALBION *	L14	15	TORBAY	S90	12
BULWARK	L15	15	TRENCHANT	S91	12
			TALENT	S92	12
Destroyers			TRIUMPH	S93	12
			ASTUTE	S119	10
DARING	D32	16	AMBUSH	S120	10
DAUNTLESS	D33	16			
DIAMOND	D34	16	**Minehunters**		
DRAGON	D35	16			
DEFENDER	D36	16	LEDBURY	M30	21
DUNCAN	D37	16	CATTISTOCK	M31	21
EDINBURGH	D97	18	BROCKLESBY	M33	21
			MIDDLETON	M34	21
Frigates			CHIDDINGFOLD	M37	21
			ATHERSTONE	M38	21
KENT	F78	19	HURWORTH	M39	21
PORTLAND	F79	19	QUORN	M41	21
SUTHERLAND	F81	19	PENZANCE	M106	23
SOMERSET	F82	19	PEMBROKE	M107	23
ST ALBANS	F83	19	GRIMSBY	M108	23
LANCASTER	F229	19	BANGOR	M109	23
ARGYLL	F231	19	RAMSEY	M110	23
IRON DUKE	F234	19	BLYTH	M111	23
MONMOUTH	F235	19	SHOREHAM	M112	23
MONTROSE	F236	19			
WESTMINSTER	F237	20	**Patrol Craft**		
NORTHUMBERLAND	F238	20			
RICHMOND	F239	20	EXPRESS	P163	27

Ship	Pennant Number	Page	Ship	Pennant Number	Page
EXPLORER	P164	27	PUNCHER	P291	28
EXAMPLE	P165	27	CHARGER	P292	28
EXPLOIT	P167	27	RANGER	P293	28
CLYDE	P257	25	TRUMPETER	P294	28
ARCHER	P264	27			
BITER	P270	27	**Survey Ships & RN Manned Auxiliaries**		
SMITER	P272	27			
PURSUER	P273	27			
TRACKER	P274	27	GLEANER	H86	31
RAIDER	P275	27	ECHO	H87	30
BLAZER	P279	27	ENTERPRISE	H88	30
DASHER	P280	27	SCOTT	H131	29
TYNE	P281	24	ENDURANCE	A171	33
SEVERN	P282	24	PROTECTOR	A173	32
MERSEY	P283	24			
SCIMITAR	P284	26	*Vessel is at extended readiness*		
SABRE	P285	26			

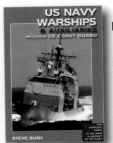

HMS Vigilant

SUBMARINES
VANGUARD CLASS

Ship	Pennant Number	Completion Date	Builder
VANGUARD	S28	1992	VSEL
VICTORIOUS	S29	1994	VSEL
VIGILANT	S30	1997	VSEL
VENGEANCE	S31	1999	VSEL

Displacement 15,980 tons (dived) **Dimensions** 149.9m x 12.8m x 12m **Speed** 25 + dived **Armament** 16 Tubes for Trident 2 (D5) missiles, 4 Torpedo Tubes **Complement** 135

Notes

After the first successful UK D5 missile firing in May '94 the first operational patrol was carried out in early '95 and a patrol has been constantly maintained ever since. The UK's Trident missiles have been de-targeted since 1994, and the submarine on deterrent patrol is normally at several days notice to fire her missiles. VENGEANCE, the final submarine to enter the refit cycle, arrived at Devonport on 2 March 2012. VIGILANT left Devonport following her refit on 27 March 2012. In 2010 the Government revealed plans to extend the service life of the Vanguard class to beyond 2028 while at the same time reducing the number of operational missiles on each submarine to just eight. To achieve the five year extension will require three additional Long Overhaul Periods (LOPs), at Devonport, costing around £1.3 billion between 2014 and 2024.

HMS Ambush

ASTUTE CLASS

Ship	Pennant Number	Completion Date	Builder
ASTUTE	S119	2009	BAE Submarine Solutions
AMBUSH	S120	2012	BAE Submarine Solutions
ARTFUL	S121	Building	BAE Submarine Solutions
AUDACIOUS	S122	Building	BAE Submarine Solutions
ANSON	S123	Building	BAE Submarine Solutions
AGAMEMNON	S124	Planned	BAE Submarine Solutions
AJAX	S125	Planned	BAE Submarine Solutions

Displacement 7,400 tonnes (7,800 dived) **Dimensions** 97m x 11.2m x 9.5m **Speed** 29+ dived **Armament** 6 Torpedo Tubes; Spearfish torpedoes; Tomahawk cruise missiles for a payload of 38 weapons **Complement** 98 (Accommodation for 12 Officers and 97 Ratings)

Notes

Ordered in 1997, the Astute class were intended, initially, to replace the S class in RN service. The first submarine, ASTUTE, was delivered in 2009 and commissioned on 27 August 2010. AMBUSH was launched (rolled out from Devonshire Hall) on 16 December 2010 and conducted her initial basin dive in October 2011. The keel for AUDACIOUS was laid on 24 May 2009 and for the fifth boat, ANSON, on 13 October 2011. Long lead procurement has begun for the sixth submarine AGAMEMNON and, although the seventh submarine, AJAX, has been confirmed, it has not yet been ordered.

The Astute class is designed to fulfil a range of key strategic and tactical roles including anti-ship and anti-submarine operations, surveillance and intelligence gathering and support for land forces. Each boat will have a lock in lock out capability, enabling swimmers to leave the submarine while dived. This capability is in addition to the Chalfont dry deck hangar which can be fitted to the aft casing and designed to hold a swimmer delivery vehicle for stand off insertion.

ASTUTE, achieved its in-service date in April 2010 and following 147 days deployed to the USA for weapon trials she returned to the UK for a period of maintenance and modifications prior to continuing her sea trials, which included operating with the Chalfont dry deck shelter embarked. She is expected to achieve full operational status in 2013. The second submarine, AMBUSH, sailed for the first time in mid-September 2012, arriving at Faslane on 19 September from where she will conduct her sea trials.

The planned in-service dates for the remainder of the Astute class boats are: ARTFUL (2015); AUDACIOUS (2018); ANSON (2020); AGAMEMNON (2022) and AJAX (2024).

HMS Tireless

TRAFALGAR CLASS

Ship	Pennant Number	Completion Date	Builder
TIRELESS	S88	1985	Vickers
TORBAY	S90	1986	Vickers
TRENCHANT	S91	1989	Vickers
TALENT	S92	1990	Vickers
TRIUMPH	S93	1991	Vickers

Displacement 4,500 tons 5,200 tons dived **Dimensions** 85.4m x 9.8m x 9.5m **Speed** 30+ dived **Armament** 5 Torpedo Tubes; Spearfish torpedoes; Tomahawk cruise missiles for a payload of 24 weapons **Complement** 130

Notes

TORBAY, TALENT, TRENCHANT and TRIUMPH have undergone upgrade and received Type 2076 Sonar. TALENT returned to service in 2012 following a 13 month refit. TORBAY is undergoing refit with work expected to complete in the summer (2013). TURBULENT has been withdrawn from service, decommissioning on 14 July 2012. Other decommissioning dates are TIRELESS (2013); TORBAY (2015); TRENCHANT (2017); TALENT (2019) and TRIUMPH (2022).

HMS Illustrious

LANDING PLATFORM HELICOPTER (LPH)

INVINCIBLE CLASS

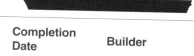

Ship	Pennant Number	Completion Date	Builder
ILLUSTRIOUS	R06	1982	Swan Hunter

Displacement 22,500 tonnes **Dimensions** 210m x 36m x 6.5m **Speed** 28 knots
Armament 2 - 20mm guns, 3 Goalkeeper **Aircraft** Tailored Air Group (Merlin, Sea King, Chinook, Apache as required) **Complement** 726 + 384 Air Group (600 troops)

Notes

With the withdrawal of the Harrier from service in April 2010 she now operates in the LPH role. She emerged from refit at Rosyth in July 2011. In October and November 2011 the ship underwent a seven week period of operational sea training to prepare her for her new role before taking over from OCEAN in early 2012. ILLUSTRIOUS is scheduled to serve in the LPH role until OCEAN completes her refit around 2014. At that time ILLUS-TRIOUS will be withdrawn from service. In 2012 the MoD, in announcing the contract to recycle ARK ROYAL, stated their wish that ILLUSTRIOUS, on decommissioning, should be preserved. The MoD are keen to seek innovative proposals from a range of organisations, including private sector companies, charities and trusts.

HMS Ocean

OCEAN

Ship	Pennant Number	Completion Date	Builder
OCEAN	L12	1998	Kvaerner

Displacement 22,500 tonnes **Dimensions** 203.8m x 35m x 6.6m **Speed** 17 knots **Armament** 3 x Phalanx, 4 x 20mm BMARC guns, 4 x Minigun **Aircraft** Tailored Air Group (Merlin, Sea King, Chinook, Apache as required) **Complement** Ship 285, Squadrons 206 (maximum 1275 including Royal Marines)

Notes

Can carry 12 Sea King and 6 Lynx helicopters. Frequently employed as the flagship of the UK Amphibious Ready Group. RAF Chinook helicopters are normally carried as an integral part of the ship's air group, but they are unable to be stowed below decks. Modified with two 50m blisters attached to the hull at the waterline below the after chine to improve safety margins while deploying LCVPs from the after davits. Vessel is somewhat constrained by her slow speed. Many improvements have been made to her including accomodation for both crew and embarked Royal Marines; advanced communications facilities; a better weapon defence system and an upgrade to the ship's aviation support facilities to improve support to helicopter operations including the Apache attack helicopter. In late 2012 she arrived at Devonport to prepare for a 12 month refit. Following sea trials and operational training it is intended that she will resume the role of LPH from ILLUSTRIOUS in 2014.

HMS Bulwark

LANDING PLATFORM DOCK (LPD)

ALBION CLASS

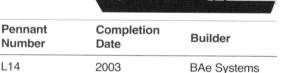

Ship	Pennant Number	Completion Date	Builder
ALBION	L14	2003	BAe Systems
BULWARK	L15	2004	BAe Systems

Displacement 18,500 tons, 21,500 tons (flooded) **Dimensions** 176m x 25.6m x 7.1m **Speed** 18 knots **Armament** 2 x CIWS, 2 x 20mm guns (single) **Complement** 325 **Military Lift** 303 troops, with an overload capacity of a further 405

Notes

Vehicle deck capacity for up to six Challenger 2 tanks or around 30 armoured all-terrain tracked vehicles. Floodable well dock able to take four utility landing craft. Four smaller landing craft carried on davits. Two-spot flight deck able to take medium support helicopters and stow a third. Flightdeck allows the simultaneous operation of two Chinook helicopters. These vessels do not have a hangar but have equipment needed to support aircraft operations. Only one of the class remains operational at this time. BULWARK assumed the role of fleet flagship in October 2011. On 23 March 2012 ALBION entered a 33-month period of extended readiness during which time she will provide training for Landing Craft Davit operations. In 2014 she will undergo a regeneration refit and rejoin the fleet in 2016.

HMS Defender

DESTROYERS
DARING CLASS
(Type 45)

Ship	Pennant Number	Completion Date	Builder
DARING	D32	2008	BVT Surface Fleet
DAUNTLESS	D33	2008	BVT Surface Fleet
DIAMOND	D34	2009	BVT Surface Fleet
DRAGON	D35	2011	BVT Surface Fleet
DEFENDER	D36	2012	BVT Surface Fleet
DUNCAN	D37	2013	BVT Surface Fleet

Displacement 7,350 tons **Dimensions** 152.4m x 21.2m x 5.7m **Speed** 29 knots **Armament** 1 - 4.5-inch gun, Sea Viper missile system comprising Sylver VLS with combination of up to 48 Aster 15 and Aster 30 missiles, 2 x Vulcan Phalanx (fitted as required) **Aircraft** Lynx or Merlin **Complement** 190 (with space for 235)

Notes

Originally to have been a class of up to 12 ships this was reduced to just six. The bow sections, funnels and masts were built at Portsmouth and then transported by barge to Govan where final assembly and fitting out takes place. DARING was commissioned on 23 July 2009 and declared operational on 31 July 2010. DAUNTLESS was handed over to the RN in December 2009 and DIAMOND on 22 September 2010. The fourth vessel

DRAGON was handed over in August 2011 and commissioned on 20 April 2012. DEFENDER arrived at Portsmouth for the first time on 25 July 2012 where she will undergo sea trials before being declared ready for operations in 2013. The final vessel, DUNCAN, commenced her initial sea trials in September 2012 and is scheduled to be handed over to the Royal Navy in 2013. In September 2009 a £309m contract was awarded to BVT Surface Fleet for the in-service support for the Type 45 class for up to seven years, starting in January 2010.

DRAGON is the first of the batch two destroyers, which include upgrades to systems onboard in line with technological developments.

In September 2010 DAUNTLESS successfully conducted the first High Seas Firing of the Sea Viper anti-air guided weapon system, the first time that the missile had been fired from a Type 45 destroyer. DARING successfully proved the system in May with her first high-seas firing.

The first three Type 45s have now conducted their maiden operational deployments. DARING returned to Portsmouth on 1 August 2012 following a deployment to the Gulf. She was relieved by her sister DIAMOND, which had departed from Portsmouth on 13 June 2012. DAUNTLESS returned to Portsmouth on 30 October 2012 following a deployment to the South Atlantic and West Africa.

HMS Edinburgh

SHEFFIELD CLASS
(Type 42) Batch 3

Ship	Pennant Number	Completion Date	Builder
EDINBURGH	D97	1985	C. Laird

Displacement 5,200 tonnes **Dimensions** 141m x 15.2m x 7m **Speed** 30 knots + **Armament** 1- 4.5-inch gun, 2 - Phalanx, 2 - 20mm guns, Sea Dart missile system, Lynx Helicopter **Complement** 287

Notes

The sole remaining Type 42 in RN service, she is a stretched version of earlier ships of this class. Designed to provide area defence of a task force. Deck edge stiffening fitted to counter increased hull stress. YORK decommissioned on 28 September 2012. EDINBURGH sailed from Portsmouth on 24 September 2012 for her final deployment. She will decommission this year (2013).

The last of the Batch II Type 42 destroyers, LIVERPOOL, decommissioned on 30 March 2012.

HMS Montrose

FRIGATES
DUKE CLASS (Type 23)

Ship	Pennant Number	Completion Date	Builder
KENT*	F78	2000	Yarrow
PORTLAND	F79	2000	Yarrow
SUTHERLAND*	F81	1997	Yarrow
SOMERSET*	F82	1996	Yarrow
ST ALBANS	F83	2001	Yarrow
LANCASTER*	F229	1991	Yarrow
ARGYLL*	F231	1991	Yarrow
IRON DUKE*	F234	1992	Yarrow
MONMOUTH*	F235	1993	Yarrow
MONTROSE*	F236	1993	Yarrow

Ship	Pennant Number	Completion Date	Builder
WESTMINSTER*	F237	1993	Swan Hunter
NORTHUMBERLAND*	F238	1994	Swan Hunter
RICHMOND*	F239	1994	Swan Hunter

Displacement 4,900 tonnes **Dimensions** 133m x 16.1m x 5m **Speed** 28 knots **Armament** Harpoon & Seawolf missile systems: 1 - 4.5-inch gun, 2 - single 30mm guns, 4 - 2 twin, magazine launched, Torpedo Tubes, Lynx or Merlin helicopter **Complement** 185

Notes

Now the sole class of frigate in RN service, the ships incorporate 'Stealth' technology to minimise magnetic, radar, acoustic and infra-red signatures. Gas turbine and diesel electric propulsion. Those ships marked * have been fitted with the Mk 8 Mod 1 4.5-inch gun. Type 2087 Sonar is to be fitted in only 9 of the remaining 13 of the class (ARGYLL, MONTROSE, MONMOUTH and IRON DUKE will not receive the upgrade). Both KENT and RICHMOND returned to the fleet in 2012 following modernisation refits during which time they received the new DNA(2) Command System and upgrades to the gun and missile systems.

In August 2008 the MoD announced that the Type 996 surveillance and target indication radar is to be replaced by the ARTISAN 3D Medium Range Radar (now designated Type 997) under a £100 million contract covering demonstration, manufacturing, delivery and the first 10 years of in-service support. The ARTISAN 3D (Advanced Radar Target Indication Situational Awareness and Navigation) is a modular open architecture maritime radar system designed to deal with complex littoral environments. It is planned to be incrementally installed between 2011 and 2015. IRON DUKE is scheduled to recieve its new radar during a refit period that commenced in March 2012. She is due to re-enter sevice in 2013.

The Seawolf missile system is expected to reach the end of its service life around 2018 and studies are underway for a replacement system. The MoD and MBDA have been involved in preliminary studies to define and develop a common solution for such anti-air target guided weapons, used for naval, land and aerial operations which could be implemented in a future system currently known as CAMM – the Common Anti-air Modular Missile, to be fielded in 2015-2018. The CAMM family is being designed to meet the MoD's requirement for a Future Local Area Air Defence System (FLAADS) for the Type 23 Frigate and, subsequently, for the Future Surface Combatant.

Under current plans ships are scheduled to decommission as follows: ARGYLL 2023; LANCASTER 2024; IRON DUKE 2025; MONMOUTH 2026; MONTROSE 2027; WESTMINSTER 2028; NORTHUMBERLAND 2029 ; RICHMOND 2030; SOMERSET 2031; SUTHERLAND 2033; KENT 2034; PORTLAND 2035 and ST. ALBANS 2036.

HMS Atherstone

MINE COUNTERMEASURES SHIPS (MCMV)
HUNT CLASS

Ship	Pennant Number	Completion Date	Builder
LEDBURY	M30	1981	Vosper T.
CATTISTOCK	M31	1982	Vosper T.
BROCKLESBY	M33	1983	Vosper T.
MIDDLETON	M34	1984	Yarrow
CHIDDINGFOLD	M37	1984	Vosper T.
ATHERSTONE	M38	1987	Vosper T.
HURWORTH	M39	1985	Vosper T.
QUORN	M41	1989	Vosper T.

Displacement 750 tonnes **Dimensions** 60m x 10.5m x 3.4m **Speed** 15 knots **Armament** 1 x 30mm + 2 x Miniguns **Complement** 45

Notes

The largest warships ever built of glass reinforced plastic. Their cost (£35m each) has dictated the size of the class. Very sophisticated ships - and lively seaboats! All are based at Portsmouth as the Second Mine Countermeasures Squadron (MCM2).

BAE Systems has been awarded a six-year contract worth £15m to replace the propulsion systems on these ships, with the work to be carried out at Portsmouth. The first new propulsion system, comprising two Caterpillar C32 engines (replacing the older Napier Deltics) has been installed on board CHIDDINGFOLD during her current refit. She is scheduled to return to service in 2013. Upgrades to the remaining seven ships will take place during planned ship docking periods up to 2016. The re-propulsion project will involve the installation of new engines, gearboxes, bow thruster systems, propellers and machinery control systems.

LEDBURY to decommission in 2019, CATTISTOCK, BROCKLESBY, CHIDDINGFOLD and MIDDLETON 2020, HURWORTH and ATHERSTONE 2022 and QUORN 2023. In order to keep up the overseas deployment tempo, crews can be swapped between ships. ATHERSTONE and QUORN are forward deployed to the Gulf. MIDDLETON returned to the UK on 31 August 2012 following a 3-year deployment to the Gulf.

HMS Blyth

SANDOWN CLASS

Ship	Pennant Number	Completion Date	Builder
PENZANCE	M106	1998	Vosper T.
PEMBROKE	M107	1998	Vosper T.
GRIMSBY	M108	1999	Vosper T.
BANGOR	M109	2000	Vosper T.
RAMSEY	M110	2000	Vosper T.
BLYTH	M111	2001	Vosper T.
SHOREHAM	M112	2001	Vosper T.

Displacement 600 tons **Dimensions** 52.5m x 109.m x 2m **Speed** 13 knots **Armament** 1 - 30mm gun; 2 x Miniguns; 3 x GPMG **Complement** 34

Notes

A class dedicated to a single mine hunting role. Propulsion is by vectored thrust and bow thrusters. All are based at Faslane as the First Mine Countermeasures Squadron (MCM1). The ships are manned by eight numbered crews which are rotated throughout the squadron allowing deployed vessels to remain on station for extended periods. RAMSEY and SHOREHAM are forward deployed to the Gulf. PEMBROKE returned to the UK on 31 August 2012 on completion of a 3-year deployment to the Gulf.

HMS Tyne

PATROL VESSELS
RIVER CLASS

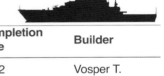

Ship	Pennant Number	Completion Date	Builder
TYNE	P281	2002	Vosper T.
SEVERN	P282	2003	Vosper T.
MERSEY	P283	2003	Vosper T.

Displacement 1,677 tonnes **Dimensions** 79.5m x 13.6m x 3.8m **Speed** 20+ knots **Armament** 1 x 20mm; 2 x GPMG **Complement** 48

Notes

Ordered on 8 May 2001, the deal was unusual in that the ships were leased from Vospers (VT) for five years under a £60 million contract. The lease arrangement appeared to have been a success with VT meeting their commitment of having the ships available for over 300 days a year. In January 2007 a £52 million lease-contract extension was awarded extending their RN service to the end of 2013. In September 2012, rather than face having to pay more to rent the vessels – £7m a year for all three – Whitehall signed a £39m contract to buy the ships outright, keeping them in service with the RN for the next ten years. The River class are now the only RN ships conducting Fishery Protection patrols in the waters around England, Wales and Northern Ireland.

HMS Clyde

BATCH II RIVER CLASS

Ship	Pennant Number	Completion Date	Builder
CLYDE	P257	2006	VT Shipbuilding

Displacement 1,847 tonnes **Dimensions** 81.5m x 13.6m x 4.15m **Speed** 19 knots (full load) 21 knots (sprint) **Aircraft** Flight Deck to take Lynx, Sea King or Merlin Helicopter **Armament** 1 - 30mm gun; 5 x GPMG; 2 x Minigun **Complement** 36 (space for additional 20 personnel - see note)

Notes

Designed to carry out patrol duties around the Falkland Islands and their dependencies, the ship is able to accommodate a single helicopter up to Merlin size. She deployed to the Falklands in August 2007. CLYDE's more modern design has enabled her to remain on task in the South Atlantic until later this year. Like the previous River class, she had been leased from BAE Systems, for a period of five years. In July 2011 it was announced that BAE Systems had been awarded a six-year contract extension to deliver support services to the ship until 2018. The annual cost to the public purse of operating the ship is £3.5 million.

CLYDE is able to embark a Military Force of up to 110 personnel (the size of the Roulement Infantry Company (RIC)) and move them around the Falkland Islands, inserting them at will.

● DANIEL FERRO   **HMS Sabre**

LIFESPAN PATROL VESSELS (LPVs)

Ship	Pennant Number	Completion Date	Builder
SCIMITAR	P284	1988	Halmatic
SABRE	P285	1988	Halmatic

Displacement 18.5 tons   **Dimensions** 16m x 4.7m x 1.4m   **Speed** 27+ knots
Armament 2 x GPMG   **Complement** 4

Notes

Purpose built in 1988 for counter terrorism duties on Lough Neagh, Northern Ireland. Operated in anonimity as GREYFOX and GREYWOLF until withdrawn from service in 2002 and transferred to Gibraltar to join the Royal Navy Gibraltar Squadron (RNGS). The Squadron comprises the two Scimitar-class patrol boats, 21 personnel, and three Pacific rigid-hulled inflatable boats. RNGS provides Force Protection to visiting coalition warships, maritime security patrols within British Gibraltar Territorial Waters and supports a variety of operations within the Joint Operating Area.

HMS Gleaner

INSHORE SURVEY VESSEL

Ship	Pennant Number	Completion Date	Builder
GLEANER	H86	1983	Emsworth

Displacement 26 tons **Dimensions** 14.8m x 4.7m x 1.6m **Speed** 14 knots
Complement 8

Notes

Small inshore survey craft used for the collection of data from the shallowest inshore waters. She uses multibeam and sidescan sonar to collect bathymetry and seabed texture data and compile an accurate and detailed picture of the seabed. She was scheduled to decommission in 2007, but she emerged, in 2008, from a Service Life Extension Programme, which will enable her to remain in service for a further 10 years. She carries the prefix Her Majesty's Survey Motor Launch or HMSML.

ICE PATROL SHIPS
PROTECTOR

Ship	Pennant Number	Completion Date	Builder
PROTECTOR	A173	2001	Havyard Leirvik (Norway)

Displacement 4,985 tons **Dimensions** 89.7m x 18m x 7.25m **Speed** 15 knots
Armament Miniguns; GPMGs **Complement** 88

Notes

The ice-breaker MV POLARBJORN was leased on a three-year contract from the Norwegian company GC Rieber Shipping as a temporary replacement for the damaged ENDURANCE. Following an intensive 10-day refit at Odense, Denmark, she sailed for Portsmouth where she was commissioned as PROTECTOR on 23 June. The contract for the lease of the ship, worth £26 million over three years, also includes full contractor support and some fitting or refurbishment of equipment for use by the RN. In addition to this, a further £3.7 million was spent to fit military task equipment such as survey boats and communications equipment. Although the ship has a flight deck, there is no hangar, so she will be unable to deploy with an embarked helicopter. She operates the Survey Motor Boat JAMES CAIRD IV and the 8.5 metre Rigid Work Boat TERRA NOVA. She can also deploy two Pacific 22 RIBs (NIMROD and AURORA). She also deploys with three BV206 all terrain vehicles and four quadbikes and trailers to assist in moving stores and equipment. She sailed for her second Antarctic season on 17 September 2012.

HMS Endurance

ENDURANCE

Ship	Pennant Number	Completion Date	Builder
ENDURANCE	A171	1990	Ulstein-Hatlo

Displacement 5,129 tons **Dimensions** 91m x 17.9m x 6.5m **Speed** 14.9 knots
Armament Small arms **Aircraft** 2 Lynx **Complement** 116

Notes

Chartered for only 7 months in late 1991 to replace the older vessel of the same name. Originally M/V POLAR CIRCLE, renamed HMS POLAR CIRCLE (A176) and then purchased by MoD(N) and renamed again in October 1992 to current name. Historically spent 4-6 months each year in the South Atlantic supporting the British Antarctic Survey. Following a flooding incident off Chile in 2008 she was returned to the UK aboard a heavylift ship in April 2009. She has remained at Portsmouth ever since.

Her future remains uncertain. There have long been rumours that she is to be returned to her former Norwegian owners, who intend to re-engine her for further civilian service, but an official announcement on the ship's future is still awaited.

Griffon 2400TD

ROYAL MARINE CRAFT

4 GRIFFON 2400TD LCAC

G.R.T. 6.8 tons **Dimensions** 13.4m x 6.8m **Speed** 35 knots **Range** 300 nm
Armament 1 x GPMG **Complement** 2 Crew; 16 fully-equipped marines.

Notes

Ordered in June 2008, these four Landing Craft Air Cushion (Light) (LCAC) have
replaced the four 2000TD(M) which were operated by 539 Assault Squadron. The
2400TD offers greater payload, performance and obstacle clearance than the earlier
craft, and centre sections of the cabin roof can be removed in order to embark two one-
tonne NATO pallets. They can be transported on a standard low loader truck or in the
hold of a C-130 Hercules aircraft. They can also operate directly from the well-deck of
RN amphibious ships. They are equipped with a 7.62mm General Purpose Machine
Gun, HF and VHF radios, radar, GPS, ballistic protection and a variety of specialised
equipment. All four entered service by the end of 2010.

SPECIALIST CRAFT

In addition to the familiar Rigid Raiding Craft and Rigid Inflatable Boats the Royal
Marines operate the Offshore Raiding Craft (ORC). It can be configured to transport up
to eight fully-equipped commandos at speeds of over 35 knots. It can also be fitted with
bullet-proof panels and weapon mountings to become a heavily-armed fire support
vessel. Other vessels available include air transportable Fast Insertion Craft (FIC) with
a speed of 55 knots in addition to advanced wave piercing designs. Swimmer Delivery
Vehicles (SDV), in reality miniature submarines, which can be deployed from dry deck
shelters on larger submarines, are also a part of the UK Special Forces inventory.

10 LCU Mk10

Pennants L1001 - L1010 **G.R.T.** 240 tons FL **Dimensions** 29.8m x 7.4m x 1.7m **Speed** 8.5 knots **Complement** 7

Notes

Ro-Ro style landing craft designed to operate from the Albion class LPDs. Ordered in 1998 from Ailsa Troon. The first two were delivered in 1999. The remainder were built by BAE Systems at Govan. Capable of lifting one Main Battle Tank or four lighter vehicles. Capacity for 120 troops. With a range of around 600 nautical miles – more if auxiliary tanks are added – is designed to operate independently for 14 days with its seven man Royal Marine crew in both arctic and tropical climates. All the crew members have bunk accommodation and there is a galley and store rooms. Rather than their pennant numbers, the vessels display alpha-numeric codes signifying their parent ship (A - ALBION; B - BULWARK, P - RM Poole).

The MOD is trialling the PACSCAT (Partial Air Cushion Supported Catamaran), a high-speed landing craft developed by Qinetiq. Between August and December 2010, the craft was put through its paces at Instow in North Devon and in Scottish waters with ALBION. Similar in dimensions to the LCU Mk10 the craft is entirely constructed out of aluminium and is designed to offer the triple benefits of speed, manoeuvrability and payload capacity. It is 30 metres in length, just under eight metres in width and is capable of carrying loads weighing up to 55 tonnes. Propulsion is provided by a pair of MJP water jets powered by MTU-made diesel engines and during trials the craft has demonstrated speeds in excess of 30 knots.

23 LCVP Mk5

Pennants 9473, 9673-9692, 9707, 9708 **G.R.T.** 25 tons FL **Dimensions** 15m x 4m x 1.5m **Speed** 20 knots **Complement** 3.

Notes

First one ordered in 1995 from Vosper Thornycroft and handed over in 1996. A further four were delivered in December 1996 to operate from OCEAN, with two more for training at RM Poole ordered in 1998. A further 16 were ordered from Babcock in 2001. The Mk 5 can lift 8 tonnes of stores or a mix of 2 tonnes and 35 troops. These vessels have a greater range, lift and speed than the Mk4s which they replaced.

In 2011 Sweden lent the UK a pair of rebuilt CBR 90 combat boats for a period of six months of trials to see if they can be loaded and unloaded from UK Amphibious Ships. The vessels have previously operated from the docks of the Albion class but had not been embarked on OCEAN. The boats were converted to enable them to be deployed by davit giving the RN the ability to deploy combat boats in support of operations in the littoral environment. A similar trial is being conducted with the Amphibious Ships of the Dutch Navy. It is not known whether the UK will buy CBR 90s or whether they will join with the Swedish Navy on joint operations.

SHIPS FOR THE FUTURE FLEET

QUEEN ELIZABETH CLASS AIRCRAFT CARRIERS

After a decade of design studies, a contract for the construction of two aircraft carriers, QUEEN ELIZABETH and PRINCE OF WALES, the largest warships to be designed and built in the UK, was signed in July 2008 between the Government and the Aircraft Carrier Alliance, an industrial group comprising BAE Systems Surface Ships, Babcock Marine, Thales and the Ministry of Defence.

The ships are being built in sections constructed by BAE Systems at Govan, Scotstoun and Portsmouth; Babcock in Rosyth and Appledore; Cammell Laird in Birkenhead and A & P, Tyne and are being assembled in Number 1 Dock at Rosyth. The dock at Rosyth has had the entrance widened from 124 feet to 138 feet. The sides were re-profiled with the removal of angled steps to make the dock floor 30 feet wider. A new overhead crane with a span of 394 feet, named Goliath, has been installed to straddle the dock and lift the smaller blocks into place. The individual blocks are built under cover and fitted out with machinery and sub-assemblies such as diesel generators, offices, cabins and galleys before they are moved to Rosyth. The first ship is now undergoing final assembly at Rosyth, with the last major hull block, the 10,000 ton LB03, having arrived at Rosyth on 11 November 2012.

The completed ships will be 284 metres long with a waterline beam of 39 metres and beam across the flight deck of 73 metres. Height from the bottom of the hull to the masthead will be 57.5 metres and draught 11 metres. There are 9 decks in the hull with another 9 in the two islands. Each ship is expected to be in the dock for two years and will be 'floated out' into the adjacent non-tidal basin for completion. The 2010 SDSR determined that the new carriers should operate the conventional F-35C 'tail-hook' variant of the Joint Strike fighter, rather than the intended F-35B VSTOL variant and be converted for 'cat & trap' operations. The Conversion Development Phase was scheduled to run to late 2012. However, concerns as to the affordability of the CV conversion prompted the MoD to reconsider the STOVL option in an attempt to finalise its PR12 budget planning round and balance the equipment programme.

According to the MoD, work undertaken had revealed that the CV-capable carrier strike capability would not be ready until 2023, some three years later than originally planned. Furthermore, the cost of fitting the Electromagnetic Aircraft Launch System (EMALS), Advanced Arresting Gear (AAG) and other CV aviation systems into PRINCE OF WALES was now estimated at £2 billion, over double the initial estimate of £950 million.

In his statement to parliament, the Secretary of State for Defence said that the SDSR decision on carriers "was right at the time, but the facts have changed and therefore so too must our approach".

He added: "Carrier strike with 'cats and traps' using the Carrier Variant jet no longer rep-resents the best way of delivering carrier strike and I am not prepared to tolerate a three year further delay to reintroducing our Carrier Strike capability." The MoD initially said that about £40 million had been spent to date on the carrier Conversion Development Phase. However, he later admitted that the total cost of the u-turn, taking into account other costs and penalties, came to about £100 million.

QUEEN ELIZABETH is due to start sea trials in 2017. The MoD stated that reverting to the F-35B would enable ship/aviation integration trials to begin in 2018, allowing an initial operating capability from sea in 2020.

TYPE 26 FRIGATE (GLOBAL COMBAT SHIP)

The Type 26 Global Combat Ship project entered its Assessment Phase in March 2010, and a four-year contract was placed with BAE Systems Surface Ships to work with the MoD to produce a full design specification to be taken into the demonstration and build phases. In August 2012 the MoD revealed the design as it announced that the Type 26 had achieve its Main Gate 1 milestone.

The Type 26 is fundamental to the RN's future force structure. With the Strategic SDSR setting the frigate/destroyer force at 19 ships, the current MoD planning assumption is for 13 multi-mission Type 26 vessels (of which eight will be enhanced with longer range anti-submarine warfare [ASW] capability) to progressively replace the current Type 23 frigates from 2021. However, a final decision on ship numbers will not be confirmed until the Main Gate 2 investment decision, planned for 2014, is taken.

The resultant Type 26 design (denoted as T26 GCS1f) is a 5,400 tonne displacement steel monohull with a length of 148 metres, a beam of 20 metres and a draught of 7.2 metres. A Combined Diesel Electric or Gas (CODLOG) machinery arrangement will provide for a maximum speed in excess of 28 kt, and a range of 7,000 n miles at 15 kt. The design features a Flexible Mission Space forward of the hangar providing a significant volume for a range of payloads - for instance, four 12 metre rigid inflatables, up to 10 containers, or a mix of unmanned vehicles. Armament will comprise a 5-inch gun, a 24-cell strike-length vertical launcher and the Sea Ceptor local area air defence system. It is anticipated that construction will begin in 2015.

MILITARY AFLOAT REACH AND SUSTAINABILITY (MARS)

The future re-equipment of the RFA rests with this programme in which it is envisioned 11 ships will be procured (Five fleet tankers - delivered 2011 to 2015; Three joint sea-based logistics vessels - 2016, 2017 and 2020; Two fleet solid-support ships - 2017 and 2020 and a single fleet tanker - 2021).

At the end of 2007 the MoD invited industry to express their interest in the project to build up to six fleet tankers. In May 2008 four companies had been shortlisted to submit proposals for the design and construction of the ships however, this project was deferred in December 2008, the MoD announcing that having reviewed all the components of the MARS fleet auxiliary programme it was concluded that there was scope for considering alternative approaches to its procurement. Post SDSR the government stated that the requirement for the MARS programme is driven by the logistic support needs of the future RN; these being assessed following the outcome of the SDSR. It now seems likely that MARS will deliver just seven vessels (four tankers and up to three solid-support ships).

In February 2012 the MoD announced that Daewoo Shipbuilding and Marine Engineering (DSME) of South Korea were the preferred bidder in a £425 million contract to build four 37,000 tonne tankers for the RFA, the first of which is planned to enter service in 2016. They will form a new Tide class, being named TIDESPRING, TIDERACE, TIDESURGE and TIDEFORCE.

The principal particulars of the design include an overall length of 200.9 metres, a breadth of 28.6 metres, a draught of 10 metres, and a displacement (full load) of just over 37,000 tonnes. Replenishment facilities comprise: three abeam RAS(L) stations (two sited starboard and one to port) for diesel oil, aviation fuel and fresh water; solid RAS reception up to 2 tonnes; and vertical replenishment using an embarked helicopter (the design features a flight deck sized for a Merlin, a maintenance hangar, and an in-flight refuelling capability). Provision is also made for the future fit of a stern fuel delivery reel. DSME is building the four ships at its Okpo shipyard on the southern island of Geoje.

With the tanker programme now under contract, the MoD is turning its attention towards the other MARS component in the shape of the Future Solid Support (FSS) programme. This second element of the modernisation of the RFA is intended to introduce replacements for RFAs FORT AUSTIN, FORT ROSALIE and FORT VICTORIA from the early 2020s.

The FSS design will deliver bulk ammunition, dry stores and food to support both carrier strike and littoral manoeuvre operations. Current plans assume a total of three FSS vessels, each displacing approximately 40,000 tonnes.

SUCCESSOR SUBMARINE PROGRAMME

The Successor programme envisages the delivery of three or four SSBNs to replace the RN's four existing Vanguard-class submarines from 2028 to maintain continuous at-sea deterrence (CASD). Initial gate approval was announced by the MoD in May 2011, marking the transition from the programme's concept phase to the current assessment phase. Assessment phase activities will finalise the Successor design, fund long lead items and start industrialisation to support manufacture. However, the key main gate investment decision - which will commit to construction and also determine whether CASD can be delivered by three or four boats - will not be taken until 2016.

Work on the concept design phase for a submarine to replace the Vanguard class has been ongoing since 2007, but this has now completed, and an outline submarine design has been selected.

In 2012 two contracts worth £350 million each were awarded by the MoD to enable detailed design work to continue on both the submarine design and the new PWR3 nuclear reactor. Although a decision on the final design and build will not be made until 2016, detailed work has to take place now to ensure that the Successor submarines can begin to be delivered in 2028.

THE ROYAL FLEET AUXILIARY

The Royal Fleet Auxiliary (RFA) is a civilian manned fleet, owned by the Ministry of Defence. Traditionally, its main task has been to replenish warships of the Royal Navy at sea with fuel, food, stores and ammunition to extend their operations away from base support. However, as the RN surface fleet has shrunk, the RFA has shrunk with it and a 'Value for Money' (VfM) review is being conducted to determine how best the support provided by the RFA can be delivered to the fleet.

Legislation banning the use of single-hulled tankers in 2010 is driving the need for replacement ships. There are three such dedicated tankers in-service with the RFA with a further general replenishment ship that has a tanking capability. However, such is the delay in the new tanker programme that the two Rover class tankers have had their service lives extended by a further seven years - making them 42 years old before they are expected to finally pay off.

As part of the Military Afloat Reach and Sustainability (MARS) programme, the MoD placed an order in 2012 for four tankers to be built in South Korea. They will be named TIDESPRING, TIDERACE, TIDESURGE and TIDEFORCE (see page 40).

The long term maintenance of the RFA fleet rests with shipyards in the North West, North East and South West of England. Cammell Laird Shiprepairers & Shipbuilders Ltd of Birkenhead and the A&P Group in Falmouth and Newcastle-upon-Tyne were named as the contractors to maintain the flotilla of 16 RFA tankers, stores and landing ships. They maintain 'clusters' of ships, providing the necessary refuelling and refit work for the RFA vessels throughout their service lives. Ships are grouped in clusters according to their duties and capabilities. A&P Group are charged with two clusters (Cluster 1: ARGUS and Cluster 2: CARDIGAN BAY, LYME BAY, MOUNTS BAY) in a contract worth around £53 million with the work to be shared between its bases in Falmouth and on the Tyne, while CL Ltd is contracted for the maintenance of four clusters of ships (Cluster 3: ORANGELEAF, BLACK ROVER, GOLD ROVER; Cluster 4: DILIGENCE, WAVE KNIGHT, WAVE RULER; Cluster 5: FORT AUSTIN, FORT ROSALIE and Cluster 6: FORT VICTORIA), with contracts totalling over £180 million. The programme is expected to save over £330 million on the previous arrangements which saw individual contracts competed for as and when they were required.

RFA Fort Rosalie

STORES VESSELS
FORT CLASS I

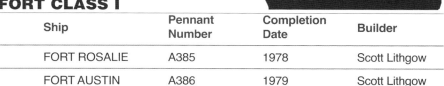

Ship	Pennant Number	Completion Date	Builder
FORT ROSALIE	A385	1978	Scott Lithgow
FORT AUSTIN	A386	1979	Scott Lithgow

Displacement 23,384 tons **Dimensions** 183m x 24m x 9m **Speed** 20 knots **Complement** 201, (120 RFA, 36 MoD Civilians & 45 Fleet Air Arm)

Notes

Full hangar and maintenance facilities are provided and up to four Sea King or Lynx helicopters can be carried for both the transfer of stores and anti-submarine protection of a group of ships (note: these ships are not cleared to operate Merlin). Both ships can be armed with 4 - 20mm guns. FORT AUSTIN began a regeneration refit in 2011 having been laid up at Portsmouth since 2009. She emerged from refit in September 2012 for trials and sea training prior to rejoining the fleet. It had been planned to decommission FORT ROSALIE in 2013 and FORT AUSTIN in 2014, but in March 2011 it was announced that these dates had been revised to 2022 and 2021 respectively.

RFA Fort Victoria

REPLENISHMENT SHIPS
FORT CLASS II

Ship	Pennant Number	Completion Date	Builder
FORT VICTORIA	A387	1992	Harland & Wolff

Displacement 35,500 tons **Dimensions** 204m x 30m x 9m **Speed** 20 knots **Armament** 4 - 30mm guns, 2 x Phalanx CIWS, Sea Wolf Missile System (Fitted for but not with) **Complement** 100 (RFA), 24 MoD Civilians, 32 RN and up to 122 Fleet Air Arm

Notes

A "One stop" replenishment ship with the widest range of armaments, fuel and spares carried. Can operate up to 5 Sea King/Lynx or 3 Merlin Helicopters (more in a ferry role) with full maintenance facilities onboard. Medical facilities were upgraded with a 12 bed surgical capability. Under current plans she is to remain in service until 2019. A sister ship, FORT GEORGE, was withdrawn from service in 2011 as part of the SDSR. She was sold for scrap in November 2012 but remains laid up at Liverpool.

RFA Mounts Bay

LANDING SHIP DOCK (AUXILIARY)
BAY CLASS

Ship	Pennant Number	Completion Date	Builder
LYME BAY	L3007	2007	Swan Hunter
MOUNTS BAY	L3008	2006	BAe Systems
CARDIGAN BAY	L3009	2007	BAe Systems

Displacement 16,190 tonnes **Dimensions** 176.6m x 26.4m x 5.1m **Speed** 18 knots **Armament** Fitted to receive in emergency **Complement** 60

Notes

The dock is capable of operating LCU 10s and they carry two LCVP Mk5s. They can offload at sea, over the horizon. In addition to their war fighting role they could be well suited to disaster relief and other humanitarian missions. MOUNTS BAY emerged from refit at the end of 2010. She now has two funnels running up the side of the midships gantry. These were resited due to problems with fumes over the aft end of the flightdeck. Additional mini-gun emplacements have been added at the stern (in place of the aft funnels) and amidships. It is unknown at this time whether this is a trial fit or if the rest of the class will receive the same level of refit. CARDIGAN BAY is deployed to the Gulf and is fitted with two Phalanx CIWS mounts. LYME BAY will return to service this year following a refit.

RFA Diligence

FORWARD REPAIR SHIP

Ship	Pennant Number	Completion Date	Builder
DILIGENCE	A132	1981	Oesundsvarvet

Displacement 10,595 tons **Dimensions** 120m x 12m x 3m **Speed** 15 knots **Armament** 2 - 20mm **Complement** RFA 40, RN Personnel - approx 100

Notes

Formerly the M/V STENA INSPECTOR purchased (£25m) for service in the South Atlantic. Her deep diving complex was removed. She is fitted with a wide range of work-shops for hull and machinery repairs, as well as facilities for supplying electricity, water, fuel, air, steam, cranes and stores to other ships and submarines. When not employed on battle repair duties she can serve as a support vessel for MCMVs and submarines on deployment. She underwent a refit in 2012 and will return to service in 2013.

CROWN COPYRIGHT/MoD 2012

RFA Argus

PRIMARY CASUALTY RECEIVING
SHIP/AVIATION TRAINING SHIP

Ship	Pennant Number	Completion Date	Builder
ARGUS	A135	1981	Cantieri Navali Breda

Displacement 28,481 tons (full load) **Dimensions** 175m x 30m x 8m **Speed** 18 knots **Armament** 4 - 30 mm, 2 - 20 mm **Complement** 254 (inc 137 Fleet Air Arm) **Aircraft** 6 Sea King/Merlin.

Notes

The former M/V CONTENDER BEZANT was purchased in 1984 and rebuilt at Harland and Wolff, Belfast, from 1984-87 to operate as an Aviation Training Ship. She undertook a rapid conversion in October 1990 to become a Primary Casualty Receiving Ship (PCRS) for service in the Gulf. These facilities were upgraded and made permanent during 2001. In 2009 the ship underwent a Service Life Extension Programme at Falmouth to switch her primary role to that of PCRS with a secondary aviation training role. The conversion has reduced helicopter capability by one landing spot and increased the efficiency of the primary care facility. Work undertaken included the construction of new casualty access lifts together with a new deckhouse aft of the superstructure; upgrade and structural modification to the bridge front; accommodation upgrades to cabins, galley & crew area; removal of starboard side vehicle ramp and installation of four additional watertight bulkheads. She has facilities for undertaking 3 major operations simultaneously, intensive care, high dependency and general wards for up to 100 patients. It also has a dentistry operating theatre, CT scanner and X-ray units. The care facility operates with a staff of up to 250 doctors, nurses and support staff. The ship is scheduled to remain in service until 2020.

MV Anvil Point

STRATEGIC SEALIFT RO-RO VESSELS
POINT CLASS

Ship	Pennant Number	Completion Date	Builder
HURST POINT		2002	Flensburger
HARTLAND POINT		2002	Harland & Wolff
EDDYSTONE		2002	Flensburger
LONGSTONE		2003	Flensburger
ANVIL POINT		2003	Harland & Wolff
BEACHY HEAD		2003	Flensburger

Displacement 10,000 tonnes, 13,300 tonnes (FL) **Dimensions** 193m x 26m x 6.6m
Speed 18 knots **Complement** 38

Notes

Foreland Shipping Limited operates these 6 ro-ro vessels built at yards in the UK and Germany under a PFI deal which was signed with the MoD on 27 June 2002 and runs until 31 December 2024. While the current main focus is on transporting equipment to and from the Middle East/Gulf in support of military activities in Afghanistan, the vessels also make regular voyages to the Falkland Islands and to Canada and Norway in support of training exercises. The six ships are all named after English lighthouses. The ships come under the operational umbrella of Defence Supply Chain Operation and Movements (DSCOM), part of the Defence Logistics Organisation.

HMS OCEAN

David Walter

US Navy

HMS DAUNTLESS

US Navy

HMS SUTHERLAND

US Navy

HMS QUORN

M41

HMS ASTUTE with Chalfont Dry Deck Shelter embarked

Brian Hargreaves

Patrick Boniface

SD VICTORIA

SD VICTORIA
LONDON
IMO 9534107

SERCO MARINE SERVICES

In December 2007 the MoD signed a £1 billion Private Finance Initiative (PFI) contract with Serco Denholm Marine Services Limited for the future provision of marine services (FPMS) over the next 15 years. In 2009 Serco bought out Denholm's share and the SD funnel logos have been replaced by a prominent Serco logo on the superstructure.

Serco manage, operate and maintain around 110 vessels used in both port and deep water operations. As part of the new contract Serco introduced 29 new vessels. The majority of these vessels have been constructed by the Netherlands based Damen Shipyards Group. Included are tugs, pilot boats and service craft. Most were selected from Damen's standard product range and fitted out to the Serco's specification. Two classes of tug, the ASD Tug 2009 and the ATD 2909, were purpose built as were the LMLBa 4315 SD OCEANSPRAY which operates with four different liquid cargoes.

Marine services embrace a wide range of waterborne and associated support activities, both in and out of port, at Portsmouth, Devonport and on the Clyde, as well as maintenance of UK and overseas moorings and navigational marks and support of a range of military operations and training.

In-port services include the provision of berthing and towage activities within the three naval bases; passenger transportation, including pilot transfers and the transportation of stores, including liquids and munitions. The recovery and disposal of waste from ships and spillage prevention and clean-up also fall within their tasking. There is also a requirement for substantial out-of-port operations. Diving training, minelaying exercises, torpedo recovery, boarding training and target towing duties are also undertaken.

The Briggs Group has been sub-contracted to assist with buoys and mooring support work. Shore based work to support these moorings and navigation buoys, have been relocated from Pembroke Dock to Burntisland on the Firth of Forth.

Initially all vessels were repainted with red funnels and hulls are now completely black, the white line having been removed as have, in most cases, the pennant numbers. All names are now prefixed with the letters 'SD' and all vessels fly the red ensign. In 2012, the last vestiges of the former RMAS identity were removed as, gradually, the whole fleet is to adopt a new colour scheme with the buff superstructure being repainted white.

SHIPS OF
SERCO MARINE SERVICES

SD Impulse

TUGS

IMPULSE CLASS

Ship	Completion Date	Builder
SD IMPULSE	1993	R. Dunston
SD IMPETUS	1993	R. Dunston

G.R.T. 400 tons approx **Dimensions** 33m x 10m x 4m **Speed** 12 knots **Complement** 5

Notes

Completed in 1993 specifically to serve as berthing tugs for the Trident Class submarines at Faslane. To be retained in service until 2022.

ASD 2509 CLASS

Ship	Completion Date	Builder
SD INDEPENDENT	2009	Damen, Gorinchem
SD INDULGENT	2009	Damen, Gorinchem

G.R.T. 345 tons approx **Dimensions** 26.09m x 9.44m x 4.3m **Speed** 13 knots
Complement Accommodation for 6. (12 passengers plus 3 crew max)

Notes

Azimuth Stern Drive (ASD) tugs. Designed for Coastal and Harbour towage, specifically modified for making cold moves within the Naval Bases. Both are based at Portsmouth.

SD Dependable

ATD 2909 CLASS

Ship	Completion Date	Builder
SD RELIABLE	2009	Damen, Stellendam
SD BOUNTIFUL	2010	Damen, Stellendam
SD RESOURCEFUL	2010	Damen, Stellendam
SD DEPENDABLE	2010	Damen, Stellendam

G.R.T. 271 tons **Dimensions** 29.14m x 9.98m x 4.8m **Speed** 13.1 knots **Complement** 3 (Accommodation for 6)

Notes

Azimuthing Tractor Drive (ATD) tugs. SD BOUNTIFUL is based at Portsmouth. SD RESOURCEFUL, SD RELIABLE and SD DEPENDABLE are based on the Clyde. Designed for Coastal and Harbour towage, specifically modified for making cold moves within the Naval Bases. Two double drum towing winches are fitted, along with extensive underwater fendering, fire fighting equipment and facilities for passenger and stores transportation.

SD Faithful

TWIN UNIT TRACTOR TUGS

Ship	Completion Date	Builder
SD ADEPT	1980	R. Dunston
SD CAREFUL	1982	R. Dunston
SD FAITHFUL	1985	R. Dunston
SD FORCEFUL	1985	R. Dunston
SD POWERFUL	1985	R. Dunston

G.R.T. 384 tons **Dimensions** 38.8m x 9.42m x 4m **Speed** 12 knots **Complement** 9

Notes

The principal harbour tugs in naval service. Some are to undergo a service life extension programme. SD POWERFUL returned to Portsmouth following a short transfer to Devonport to back fill any refit downtime for existing vessels. CAPABLE removed from service in 2011 and put up for sale at Gibraltar. SD DEXTEROUS and SD NIMBLE sold for further service in Africa as AGILITY and NIMBLE.

SD Jupiter

STAN TUG 2608 CLASS

Ship	Completion Date	Builder
SD HERCULES	2009	Damen, Gorinchem
SD JUPITER	2009	Damen, Gorinchem
SD MARS	2009	Damen, Gorinchem

G.R.T. 133.92 tons **Dimensions** 26.61m x 8.44m x 4.05m **Speed** 12 knots
Complement 4 (6 max)

Notes

A conventional Twin Screw Tug design. SD HERCULES and SD MARS are based at
Devonport. SD JUPITER is based on the Clyde. All can be used to handle submarine
mounted Towed Arrays.

SD Eileen

ASD 2009 CLASS

Ship	Completion Date	Builder
SD CHRISTINA	2010	Damen, Gdynia
SD DEBORAH	2010	Damen, Gdynia
SD EILEEN	2010	Damen, Gdynia
SD SUZANNE	2010	Damen, Gdynia

G.R.T. 120.74 tons **Dimensions** 21.2m x 9.4m x 3.6m **Speed** 11 knots **Complement** 5

Notes

Azimuth Stern Drive tugs derived from the successful Damen ASD 2411 shiphandling tug. Winches fore and aft, together with a bow thruster, make these tugs suitable for handling smaller surface ship, barge work and assisting with submarine movements. SD EILEEN and SD CHRISTINA are based at Devonport, SD SUZANNE and SD DEBORAH at Portsmouth.

SD Florence

FELICITY CLASS

Ship	Completion Date	Builder
SD FLORENCE	1980	R. Dunston
SD FRANCES	1980	R. Dunston
SD GENEVIEVE	1980	R. Dunston
SD HELEN	1974	R. Dunston

G.R.T. 88.96 tons **Dimensions** 22.0m x 6.4m x 2.6m **Speed** 10 knots **Complement** 4

Notes

Water Tractors used for the movement of small barges and equipment. Two sister vessels (GEORGINA and GWENDOLINE) sold to Serco Denholm in 1996 for service in H M Naval bases. To eventually be replaced by ASD 2009 class.

SD Catherine

PUSHY CAT 1204

Ship	Completion Date	Builder
SD CATHERINE	2008	Damen, Gorinchem
SD EMILY	2008	Damen, Gorinchem

G.R.T. 29.4 tons **Dimensions** 12.3m x 4.13m x 1.55m **Speed** 8 knots **Complement** 3

Notes

Powered by a single Caterpillar 3056 TA diesel driving a single screw. A propulsion nozzle is fitted, and twin rudders to give a 2.1 tons bollard pull. SD CATHERINE is based at Portsmouth, SD EMILY at Devonport. General line runner and harbour workboat.

SD Tilly

STAN TUG 1405

Ship	Completion Date	Builder
SD TILLY	2009	Damen, Gorinchem

G.R.T. 45 tons **Dimensions** 14.55m x 4.98m x 1.8m **Speed** 9 knots **Complement** 3

Notes

A general purpose inshore and harbour tug based at Devonport. A twin screw version of the Pushy Cat 1204. Slightly larger with a bow thruster and also developing 8 tonnes bollard pull. Line handler, general workboat and ideal for moving small barges.

SD Victoria

WORLDWIDE SUPPORT VESSEL

Ship	Completion Date	Builder
SD VICTORIA	2010	Damen, Galatz

G.R.T. 3,522 tons **Dimensions** 83m x 16m x 4.5m **Speed** 14 knots **Complement** 16 (Accommodation for 72)

Notes

Powered by two Caterpillar 3516B diesels driving two shafts with controllable pitch propellers SD VICTORIA is designed to support training operations around the world. Capable of transporting both personnel and equipment and supporting diving operations. She is equipped with classrooms, briefing rooms and operations rooms in addition to workshop facilities. There is provision to carry and operate RIBs and there is a helicopter winching deck. The former SD NEWTON arrived at Ghent, Belgium in August 2012 for breaking up.

SD Warden

TRIALS VESSEL

Ship	Completion Date	Builder
SD WARDEN	1989	Richards

Displacement 626 tons **Dimensions** 48m x 10m x 4m **Speed** 15 knots **Complement** 11

Notes

Built as a Range Maintenance Vessel but now based at Kyle of Lochalsh and operated in support of BUTEC. Also operates as a Remotely Operated Vehicle (ROV) platform. A replacement ROV has been installed and set to work to replace the older system. To remain in service until 2022.

SD Kyle of Lochalsh

TRIALS VESSEL

Ship	Completion Date	Builder
SD KYLE OF LOCHALSH	1997	Abel, Bristol

Displacement 120 tons **Dimensions** 24.35m x 9m x 3.45m **Speed** 10.5 knots **Complement** 4

Notes

The former twin screw tug MCS LENIE which has now been purchased from Maritime Craft Services (Clyde) Ltd by Serco Marine Services. The 24.35m tug, built in 1997 by Abel in Bristol, is powered by Caterpillar main engines producing a total of 2,200bhp for a bollard pull of 26 tons. She is used to support trials and operations at Kyle.

A further trials craft, SARA MAATJE V, is on long term charter from Van Stee of Holland to assist with various tasks at the Kyle of Lochalsh facility.

SD Bovisand

TENDERS
STORM CLASS

Ship	Completion Date	Builder
SD BOVISAND	1997	FBM (Cowes)
SD CAWSAND	1997	FBM (Cowes)

G.R.T 225 tonnes **Dimensions** 23m x 11m x 2m **Speed** 15 knots **Complement** 5

Notes

These craft are used in support of Flag Officer Sea Training (FOST) at Plymouth to transfer staff quickly and comfortably to and from Warships and Auxiliaries within and beyond the Plymouth breakwater in open sea conditions. These are the first vessels of a small waterplane area twin hull (SWATH) design to be ordered by the Ministry of Defence and cost £6.5 million each. Speed restrictions implemented due to wash problems generated by these vessels. To remain in service until 2022.

SD Netley

NEWHAVEN CLASS

Ship	Completion Date	Builder
SD NEWHAVEN	2000	Aluminium SB
SD NUTBOURNE	2000	Aluminium SB
SD NETLEY	2001	Aluminium SB

Tonnage 77 tonnes (45 grt) **Dimensions** 18.3m x 6.8m x 1.88m **Speed** 10 knots **Complement** 3 Crew (60 passengers)

Notes

MCA Class IV Passenger Vessels acquired as replacements for Fleet tenders. Employed on general passenger duties within the port area. To remain in service until 2022. SD NETLEY and NUTBOURNE are based at Portsmouth, NEWHAVEN at Devonport.

SD Padstow

PADSTOW CLASS

Ship	Completion Date	Builder
SD PADSTOW	2000	Aluminium SB

Tonnage 77 tonnes (45 grt) **Dimensions** 18.3m x 6.8m x 1.88m **Speed** 10 knots **Complement** 3 Crew (60 passengers)

Notes

MCA Class IV, VI and VIA Passenger Vessel based at Devonport. Used on liberty runs in Plymouth Sound and the Harbour as well as occasionally supporting FOST. To remain in service until 2022.

● JOHN CRAE

SD Oronsay

OBAN CLASS

Ship	Completion Date	Builder
SD OBAN	2000	McTay
SD ORONSAY	2000	McTay
SD OMAGH	2000	McTay

G.R.T 199 tons **Dimensions** 27.7m x 7.30m x 3.75m **Speed** 10 knots **Complement** 5 Crew (60 passengers)

Notes

MCA Class IIA Passenger Vessels which replaced Fleet tenders in 2001. SD OBAN was transferred to Devonport in 2003 and is now primarily used to support FOST staff. SD ORONSAY and SD OMAGH employed on general passenger duties on the Clyde and are additionally classified as Cargo Ship VIII(A). To remain in service until 2022.

SD Norton

PERSONNEL FERRY

Ship	Completion Date	Builder
SD NORTON	1989	FBM Marine

G.R.T 21 tons **Dimensions** 15.8m x 5.5m x 1.5m **Speed** 13 knots **Complement** 2

Notes

The single FBM catamaran, 8837, operated at Portsmouth. Can carry 30 passengers or 2 tons of stores. Was a prototype catamaran designed to replace older Harbour Launches but no more were ordered.

SD Eva

PERSONNEL FERRY

Ship	Completion Date	Builder
SD EVA	2009	Damen

G.R.T 168 tons **Dimensions** 33.21m x 7.4m x 3.3m **Speed** 23.4 knots **Complement** 4-6 (plus 34 passengers)

Notes

Operated on the Clyde as a Fast Crew Transport. With an Axe Bow design she has replaced SD ADAMANT. The Axe Bow design allows the vessel to effectively cut through waves with minimal movement of the vessel. The vessel is the first of its type in the UK to be operated under the International Code of Safety for High Speed Craft (HSC Code).

• MICHAEL LENNON

SD Meon

FLEET TENDERS

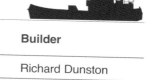

Ship	Completion Date	Builder
SD MELTON	1981	Richard Dunston
SD MENAI	1981	Richard Dunston
SD MEON	1982	Richard Dunston

G.R.T. 117.3 tons **Dimensions** 24m x 6.7m x 3.05m **Speed** 10.5 knots **Complement** 4/5 (12 passengers)

Notes

The last three survivors of a once numerous class of vessels used as Training Tenders, Passenger Ferries, or Cargo Vessels. MENAI and MEON are operated at Falmouth. MELTON is operated at Kyle. A vessel replacement programme now seems unlikely and this elderly trio are expected to remain in service until 2022.

SD Teesdale

COASTAL OILER

Ship	Completion Date	Builder
SD TEESDALE	1976	Yorkshire Drydock Co.

G.R.T. 499 tons **Dimensions** 43.86m x 9.5m x 3.92m **Speed** 8 knots **Complement** 5

Notes

Formerly the oil products tanker TEESDALE H operated by John H Whitaker. Operates as a parcel tanker delivering diesel and aviation fuel and also delivering / receiving compensating water. She is self propelled by two Aquamaster thrusters.

A Diesel Lighter Barge, SD OILMAN, was delivered to the Clyde in late November 2009 and a Water Lighter Barge, SD WATERPRESS, was delivered in November 2010, also for operation on the Clyde. A further barge, a Liquid Mixed Lighter Barge, SD OCEANSPRAY, was delivered in June 2010 and is based at Portsmouth. The elderly tanker SD OILPRESS and the water tanker SD WATERMAN are to be withdrawn from service.

SD Northern River

MULTI-PURPOSE VESSEL

Ship	Completion Date	Builder
SD NORTHERN RIVER	1998	Myklebust (Norway)

G.R.T 3,605 tons **Dimensions** 92.8m x 18.8m x 4.9m **Speed** 14 knots **Complement** 14

Notes

Bought from Deep Ocean AS (a subsidiary of Trico Marine) this Ulstein UT-745L designed Support Vessel entered service with Serco in March 2012. She can be employed on a variety of tasking from target towing, through noise ranging to data gathering; boarding training to submarine escort. Her extensive flat work deck allows her to embark containers for passive sonar training. She can also provide nuclear emergency support as well as support to submarine emergencies. In September she deployed to the Mediterranean with the NATO Submarine Rescue System embarked. She can also support the Submarine Parachute Assistance Group.

SD Moorfowl

DIVING SUPPORT VESSELS
MOOR CLASS

Ship	Completion Date	Builder
SD MOORFOWL	1989	McTay Marine
SD MOORHEN	1989	McTay Marine

Displacement 518 tons **Dimensions** 32m x 11m x 2m **Speed** 8 knots **Complement** 10

Notes

Designed as a powered mooring lighter for use within sheltered coastal waters the lifting horns have been removed from the bows of both vessels when they were converted to Diving Support Vessels. They are used by the Defence Diving School for diving training in the Kyle of Lochalsh. To remain in service until 2022.

The former SD SALMOOR and SD SALMAID were sold in 2012 and renamed KOMMANDER IONA and KOMMANDER CALUM respectively. They were towed to Poland in 2012 to undergo conversion prior to further civilian service. SD TORNADO was sold in 2012 to a German concern while SD TORMENTOR was moved to Swansea where she was broken up.

82

SD Navigator

MULTICAT 2510 CLASS

Ship	Completion Date	Builder
SD NAVIGATOR	2009	Damen, Hardinxveld
SD RAASAY	2010	Damen, Hardinxveld

G.R.T 150.27 tons **Dimensions** 26.3m x 10.64m x 2.55m **Speed** 8 knots
Complement Accommodation for 6 (plus 9 passengers)

Notes

SD NAVIGATOR is equipped for buoy handling with a single 9 ton capacity crane. She is capable of supporting diving operations. SD RAASAY was delivered on 1 January 2010 and based at the Kyle of Lochalsh. She is fitted with two cranes for torpedo recovery and support diving training. SD NAVIGATOR is managed from Portsmouth, but operates between Devonport and Portsmouth. Two similar vessels, SD INSPECTOR (ex-DMS EAGLE) and SD ENGINEER operate from Portsmouth and Devonport respectively.

SD Solent Racer

STAN TENDER 1505 CLASS

Ship	Completion Date	Builder
SD CLYDE RACER	2008	Damen, Gorinchem
SD SOLENT RACER	2008	Damen, Gorinchem
SD TAMAR RACER	2008	Damen, Gorinchem

Displacement 100 tons **Dimensions** 16m x 4.85m x 1.25m **Speed** 20 knots
Complement 3 (+ 10 Passengers)

Notes

Of aluminium construction these boats are employed on transfer of pilots, port security operations and passenger and VIP transportation. CLYDE RACER delivered 20 June 2008; SOLENT RACER 19 September 2008 and TAMAR RACER 10 December 2008.

SD Solent Spirit

STAN TENDER 1905 CLASS

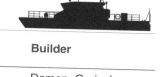

Ship	Completion Date	Builder
SD CLYDE SPIRIT	2008	Damen, Gorinchem
SD SOLENT SPIRIT	2008	Damen, Gorinchem
SD TAMAR SPIRIT	2008	Damen, Gorinchem

Displacement 100 tons **Dimensions** 18.91m x 5.06m x 1.65m **Speed** 21.7 knots **Complement** 3 (+ 10 passengers)

Notes

Steel hull with aluminium superstructure. Special propeller tunnels are fitted to increase propulsion efficiency and to reduce vibration and noise levels. These vessels are able to operate safely and keep good performance in wind speeds up to Force 6 and wave heights of 2 metres. Employed on transfer of pilots, VIPs and personnel. SD CLYDE SPIRIT delivered 27 June 2008; SD SOLENT SPIRIT 25 July 2008 and SD TAMAR SPIRIT delivered on 17 October 2008.

Kingdom of Fife

ANCHOR HANDLING TUG

Ship	Completion Date	Builder
KINGDOM OF FIFE	2008	Damen, Galatz

Displacement 1,459 tons **Dimensions** 61.2m x 13.5m x 4.75m **Speed** 13.7 knots **Complement** 18

Notes

Briggs Marine won a £100m contract from Serco to support navigation buoy maintenance and mooring support for the Royal Navy for the next 15 years. During the contract period, Briggs Marine provide support for over 350 moorings, navigation buoys and targets for the RN all around the UK coast, as well as Cyprus, Gibraltar and the Falkland Islands. KINGDOM OF FIFE was delivered in May 2008 and supports the existing Briggs Marine shallow draught and heavy lift craft CAMERON in servicing the contract, and is equipped with a decompression chamber and its own dedicated dive support team.

• JOHN NEWTH

Smit Don

AIRCREW TRAINING VESSELS

Ship	Comp Date	Builder	Base Port
SMIT DEE	2003	BES Rosyth	Buckie
SMIT DART	2003	BES Rosyth	Plymouth
SMIT DON	2003	BES Rosyth	Blyth
SMIT YARE	2003	FBMA Cebu	Great Yarmouth
SMIT TOWY	2003	FBMA Cebu	Pembroke Dock
SMIT SPEY	2003	FBMA Cebu	Plymouth

G.R.T. 95.86 GRT **Dimensions** 27.6m x 6.6m x 1.5m **Speed** 21 knots **Complement** 6

Notes

The service for Marine Support to Ranges and Aircrew Training is provided by SMIT (Scotland) Ltd and runs until April 2017. These vessels provide training for military air-crew in marine survival techniques, helicopter winching drills, target towing and general marine support tasks. More recently they have participated in Navy Command boarding exercises, simulating arms and drug smuggling activities and force protection exercises involving both Fast Attack Craft and Fast Inshore Attack Craft. SMIT DART completed as a passenger vessel with a larger superstructure. A similar, second-hand vessel, SMIT TAMAR is employed in a similar role.

Smit Stour & Smit Rother

RANGE SAFETY VESSELS

Ship	Comp Date	Builder
SMIT STOUR	2003	Maritime Partners Norway
SMIT ROTHER	2003	Maritime Partners Norway
SMIT ROMNEY	2003	Maritime Partners Norway
SMIT CERNE	2003	Maritime Partners Norway
SMIT FROME	2003	Maritime Partners Norway
SMIT MERRION	2003	Maritime Partners Norway
SMIT PENALLY	2003	Maritime Partners Norway
SMIT WEY	2003	Maritime Partners Norway
SMIT NEYLAND	2003	Maritime Partners Norway

G.R.T. 7.0 tons **Dimensions** 12.3m x 2.83m x 0.89m **Speed** 35 knots **Complement** 2

Notes

A class of 12 metre Fast Patrol Craft which operate on Range Safety Duties at Dover, Portland and Pembroke. Have replaced the former RCT Sir and Honours class launches in this role.

RCTV Arezzo

RAMPED CRAFT LOGISTIC

Vessel	Pennant Number	Completion Date	Builder
ARROMANCHES	L105	1987	James & Stone
ANDALSNES	L107	1984	James & Stone
AACHEN	L110	1986	James & Stone
AREZZO	L111	1986	James & Stone
AUDEMER	L113	1987	James & Stone

Displacement 290 tonnes (Laden) **Dimensions** 33.3m x 8.3m x 1.5m **Speed** 10 knots **Complement** 6.

Notes

Operated by the Army's 17 Port and Maritime Regiment, Royal Logistic Corps, these all purpose landing craft are capable of carrying up to 96 tons. They are self sustaining for around five days or a thousand nautical miles before requiring replenishment either at sea or in a haven. In service in UK coastal waters. ANDALSNES is operated by 417 Maritime Troop at Cyprus. ARROMANCHES was formerly AGHEILA (re-named 1994 when original vessel was sold). Most vessels sport a green and black camouflage scheme.

LOCKHEED MARTIN

Lockheed Martin LIGHTNING FRS1

Role Strike, fighter and reconnaissance aircraft
Engine 1 x Pratt & Whitney F-135 turbofan rated at 43,000lb thrust with reheat
Span 51' 4" **Length** 35' **Height** 15'
Max Weight 60,000 lbs
Max Speed Mach 1.6
Crew 1 pilot
Avionics AN/APG-81 electronically scanned radar; electro-optical targeting system; distributed aperture vision system; AN/ASQ-239 'Barracuda' electronic warfare system; helmet-mounted display system; multi-function advanced data link.
Armament Up to 12,000lb of weapons can be carried in 2 internal bays and 7 optional, external stations, a total of 11 hard-points. In 'stealth' operations the internal weapons bays can each carry one 1,000lb bomb equivalent strike weapon and a single AIM-120 AMRAAM. US versions can carry the B61-11 free-fall nuclear bomb internally as an alternative. When stealth is not required, the external pylons can be fitted to carry drop tanks and the complete inventory of USN and USMC strike weapons. Software changes to facilitate the carriage of British weapons are planned
Squadron Service The first British Lightning, ZM 135, joined 33 Fighter Wing, the JSF 'School' at Eglin Air Force Base, Florida in late 2012 to be used for training and development tasks.

Notes

The UK Government decided in mid 2012 to procure the STOVL variant of the Joint Strike Fighter, designated F-35B in the USA, instead of the F-35C carrier variant announced in the 2010 SDSR. The type's defining role is to strike at targets that have sophisticated air defences, using 'stealth' to penetrate them. It is also capable of flying fighter and reconnaissance missions but the choice of weapons is severely limited in 'stealth' mode. Three development and a single production aircraft had been ordered by the UK by late 2012, with further incremental orders planned. The first aircraft was accepted in July 2012; all will operate with British personnel in the USA until development and training to operational standards are completed.

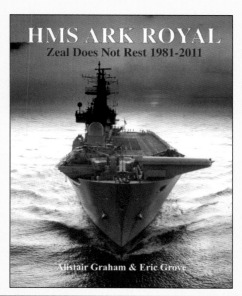

AgustaWestland MERLIN HM1, HM2

Role Anti-submarine and Maritime surveillance
Engine 3 x Rolls-Royce Turbomeca RTM322 turboshafts each developing 2,100 shp
Length 74' 10" **Width** 14' 10" **Height** 21' 10" **Main Rotor Diameter** 61'
Max Weight 32,120 lbs
Max Speed 167 kts   **Range** 625 nm
Crew 1 or 2 pilots, 1 observer and 1 sensor operator
Avionics Blue Kestrel 360 degree radar; Orange Reaper ESM; Folding Light Acoustic System for Helicopters (FLASH); AQS 903A acoustic processor; defence aids including directional infrared counter-measures (DIRCM), AN/AAR-57 missile approach warning system, chaff and flare dispensers; Wescam MX-15 electro-optical/IR camera fitted to a number of deployed aircraft.
Armament 1 x M3M 0.5" gun in cabin door; 1 x GPMG in cabin window; up to 4 Stingray torpedoes; up to 4 Mark 10 depth charges.
Squadron Service 814, 820, 824, 829 Naval Air Squadrons

Notes

Release to service trials for the HM 2 were completed and full-scale production began in 2012 with the last converted aircraft due to be delivered to the RN in December 2014. HM 2s will be issued to squadrons from 2013 with initial operational capability due in 2014. 814 and 820 NAS have 6 aircraft and 11 crews, each comprising a pilot, observer and sensor operator. 829 NAS provides flights for frigates which each have two-pilot crews. The HM 2 will differ in having a second observer in place of the sensor operator. All are based at RNAS Culdrose with 824 NAS, the training unit, when not embarked.

AgustaWestland MERLIN HC3 and planned HC4

Role Commando assault, load-lifting and tactical helicopter operations
Engine 3 x Rolls-Royce Turbomeca RTM322 turboshafts each developing 2,100 shp
Length 74' 10" **Width** 14' 10" **Height** 21' 10" **Main Rotor Diameter** 61'
Max Weight 32,120 lbs
Max Speed 167 kts **Range** 625 nm
Crew 1 or 2 pilots, 1 observer and 1 sensor operator
Avionics Defensive aids suite including directional IR counter-measures, AN/AAR-57 missile approach warning system, automatic chaff & flare dispensers; Wescam MX-15 electro-optical/IR camera
Armament 1 x M3M 0.5" gun in cabin door; 1 x 7.62mm GPMG in cabin window.
Squadron Service Commando squadrons are due to be gradually re-equipped with the type

Notes

RN personnel began training on the HC 3 in 2012 as an interim type pending a Life Sustainment Programme which will modify the aircraft to HC4 standard. This will standardise equipment with the HM 2 wherever possible and use common training and logistic support arrangements. It will have the same 'glass' cockpit and power-folding main rotor-head as the HM 2 and a new folding tail pylon above the rear-loading ramp. Flotation gear, lashing points and telebrief equipment will also be installed. Both variants can carry up to 24 marines in crash-resistant seating or a disposable load of up to 8,800lb

AgustaWestland SEA KING

Sea Kings are to be withdrawn from service by 2016. By then the type will have been in service with the RN for forty-seven years and earned the respect of generations of aircrew and maintenance engineers. The different versions will be replaced in different ways by different types.

Engines 2 x 1600shp Rolls Royce Gnome H 1400 – 1 free power turbines.
Length 54' 9" **Height** 17' 2" **Max Weight** 21,400lb **Rotor Diameter** 62' 0"
Max Speed 125 knots (HC 4+ 145 knots).

• NICK NEWNS

HAR 5

Roles Utility; COD (Carrier Onboard Delivery); SAR, aircrew training
Crew 2 pilots, 1 observer and 1 aircrewman/winchman.
Avionics Sea Searcher radar; Star Safire III EO/IR camera turret.
Armament A 7.62mm machine gun can be mounted in the doorway if required.
Squadron Service 771 Naval Air Squadron

Notes

SAR coverage in the south-western UK is provided by 771 NAS based at RNAS Culdrose. The unit also provides conversion training for ASaC and utility Sea King aircrew and maintainers. A detachment of 3 aircraft operates from Prestwick, covering a vast area of Scotland, Northern Ireland and 200 miles out into the Atlantic. By 2016 the UK SAR task is to be carried out by contracted civilian helicopters and the HAR5 is to be withdrawn from service.

ASaC 7

Role Airborne Surveillance and Control of both maritime and land operations.
Crew 1 pilot and 2 observers.
Avionics Cerberus mission-system; Searchwater radar; Orange Crop ESM; Joint Tactical Information Distribution System (Link 16). AN/AAR-57 missile approach warning system; IR jammer, radar-warning receiver; auto chaff and flare dispenser.
Squadron Service 849, 854, 857 Naval Air Squadrons.

Notes

854 and 857 NAS alternate to maintain continuous detachments in Afghanistan which provide wide area surveillance of moving objects as small as people over land and data-link the information to coalition forces. The deployed aircraft are modified with 'Carson' rotor blades, a five-bladed tail rotor and enhanced engine software which give a 30% increase in performance in 'hot and high' conditions. 849 NAS has a training role and all three squadrons are shore-based at RNAS Culdrose. The Cerberus mission system meets current requirements but the ASaC7 airframes are the oldest in RN service and due to be withdrawn from service in 2016. The MOD has yet to state clearly how their vital task is to be continued giving rise to fears that there will be a capability-gap.

HC 4

Role Commando assault, load-lifting and tactical helicopter operations.
Crew 1 or 2 pilots and 1 aircrewman. About 25% of pilots and all aircrewmen are Royal Marines.
Avionics AN/AAR-57 missile approach warning system; IR jammer; automatic chaff & flare dispenser
Armament 1 x M3M 0.5" gun in cargo door and 1 x 0.762mm GPMG in crew-entry door to give 360 degree sweeping fire when needed
Squadron Service 845, 846 and 848 Naval Air Squadrons.

Notes

The HC 4 is scheduled to be withdrawn from service in 2016 and there may be a reduction in numbers and capability as the change to the Merlin and its life sustainment programme are implemented. 845, 846 and 848 NAS are shore-based at RNAS Yeovilton but available to embark as part of a Tailored Air Group (TAG) in the operational LPH. The latter combines operational capability with a training role but all are capable of operation ashore or afloat world-wide at short notice. The Commando Helicopter Force forms part of the UK Joint Helicopter Force and operates regularly with Army and RAF helicopters both as part of a TAG and ashore.

AgustaWestland LYNX

Variants HMA 8 (SRU), AH 9A.

Roles Surface search and strike; anti-submarine strike; boarding party support; light reconnaissance and troop carrying.

Engines 2 x Rolls-Royce Gem BS 360-07-26 free power turbines each developing 900 shp.

Length 39' 1" **Height** 11' 0" **Max Weight** 9,500lb **Rotor diameter** 42' 0"

Max Speed 150 knots

Crew 1 pilot and 1 observer (AH9 1 pilot and 1 aircrewman)

Avionics : Sea Spray radar; Orange Crop ESM; Sea Owl Electro-Optical/Infrared camera (HMA 8); Second-generation Anti-jam Tactical UHF Radio for NATO (SATURN) including Successor IFF and Digital Signal processor. **Armament** External pylons for up to 4 Sea Skua ASM or 2 Stingray torpedoes. 1 door mounted M3M 0.5" gun and 1 hand-held Heckler & Koch G 3 sniper rifle to provide Precision Anti-Personnel Sniping (PAPS) in support of boarding parties in case they are opposed.

Squadron Service 702, 815 and 847 Naval Air Squadrons.

Notes

815 NAS provides operational flights to a variety of warships and RFAs; DARING class destroyers embark 2 Lynx, other ships 1. 702 NAS is a training unit with operational capability and 847 NAS operates the AH 9 in the light reconnaissance role as part of the Commando Helicopter Force; its aircraft are distinctive in having 'ROYAL MARINES' rather than 'ROYAL NAVY' painted on their sides and they carry Hellfire missiles and a door-mounted M3M 0.5" machine gun in the light strike role. The last Lynx are to be withdrawn after 2015 when the replacement Wildcat becomes operational

AgustaWestland WILDCAT

Variants AH 1, HMA 2.
Roles Maritime Search and Strike; Boarding Party Support.
Engines: 2 x LHTEC CTS 800 turboshafts each rated at 1362shp
Length 50' 0" **Height** 12' 0" **Max Weight** 13,200lb **Rotor diameter** 42' 0"
Max Speed 157 knots **Crew** 1 pilot and 1 observer.
Avionics Selex-Galileo Sea Spray 7400E multi-mode Active Electronically Scanned Array, AESA, radar; Wescam MX-15 EO/IR camera. Defensive aids suite.
Armament Future air-to-surface guided weapon in both light and heavy versions; Stingray torpedoes; Mark 11 depth-charges; door mounted M3M 0.5" gun.
Squadron Service 700W Naval Air Squadron.

Notes

The first of the 28 production HMA 2 versions for the RN was delivered during 2012 and a clearance to operate from ships' decks is due to be issued in 2013. Development work by 700W NAS will continue until full operational capability is achieved in 2015 when the type is due to replace the Lynx in operational flights. 847 NAS will be the first operational unit to re-equip with the military AH 1 version in 2014, after its return from planned operations in Afghanistan. Under present plans all versions of the Wildcat are to be based at RNAS Yeovilton and 700W is a joint unit.

TAILORED AIR GROUPS

ILLUSTRIOUS, OCEAN and big-deck RFAs operate Tailored Air Groups (TAG) comprising helicopters embarked for specific operations. They can also operate allied helicopters when necessary alongside British types. For example, during NATO operations against Libyan forces in 2011 OCEAN operated Army Apache AH1 attack helicopters; RN Sea King ASaC7 surveillance and control helicopters and US Black Hawk long-range combat SAR helicopters in case it proved necessary to recover downed aircrew from deep inside enemy territory. ILLUSTRIOUS is capable of embarking USMC, Spanish, Italian or even Thai Harriers but her ship's company would need time to work up before they could be operated efficiently.

FIXED WING OPERATIONS

SDSR 2010 left the RN with no fixed-wing fighter squadrons in commission for the first time since 1914 but the knowledge of how to operate them at sea must be kept alive to generate effective squadrons of Lightnings for QUEEN ELIZABETH and PRINCE OF WALES. This is being achieved by close co-operation with the US Navy which is allowing a number of RN pilots to train in the USA and fly F/A-18Es from US carrier decks. A small number are also expected to operate with the French Navy which is generously making slots in its carrier CHARLES de GAULLE available. The USN is providing training and slots for aircraft handlers, aircraft maintainers, air traffic control officers, meteorologists and operations officers in its carriers.

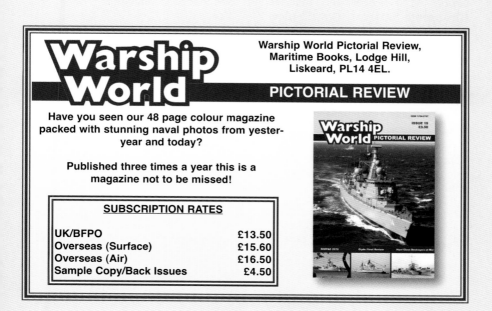

AgustaWestland APACHE

Variants AH 1
Role Attack and reconnaissance helicopter.
Engines 2 x Rolls Royce/Turbomeca RTM 322 turboshafts.
Length 58' 3" **Height** 15' 3" **Max Weight** 15,075lb **Rotor Diameter** 17' 2"
Max Speed 150 knots **Crew:** 2 pilots
Avionics Helicopter Integrated Defensive Aids Suite (HIDAS); Longbow radar, optical and infra-red target acquisition sensors.
Armament Up to 16 AGM 114 Hellfire anti-tank guided weapons; up to 4 Sidewinder air-to-air missiles; M230 30mm cannon with 1,160 rounds (chain gun); up to 76 CRV 7 unguided rockets.
Operator Operated by the Army Air Corps as part of the Joint Helicopter Force.

Notes

Apaches embark regularly in the operational LPH as part of a TAG and have considerable potential for littoral light strike operations as well as providing support for amphibious forces and escort for assault helicopters.

Boeing CHINOOK

Variants HC 2
Role Battlefield transport helicopter.
Engines 2 x 3,750 shp Avco Lycoming T55-L-712 turboshafts.
Length 98' 9" **Height** 18' 8" **Max Weight** 50,000lb **Rotor Diameter** 60' 0"
Max Speed 160 knots **Crew** 2 pilots, 1 aircrewman.
Avionics Infra-red jammer; chaff & flare dispenser, missile warning system.
Armament Up to 2 x M 134 miniguns and 1 x M 60 machine gun.
Operator Operated by the RAF as part of the Joint Helicopter Force.

Notes

The UK Joint Helicopter Force's largest and most capable helicopter, Chinooks can embark in the operational LPH but lack power-folding for their rotor blades and cannot be struck down into the hangar. QUEEN ELIZABETH will be able to strike down fully-spread Chinooks on her side lifts to stow them in the hangar and her deck is big enough to operate them in significant numbers when necessary, without interfering with other aircraft operations.

OTHER AIRCRAFT TYPES IN ROYAL NAVY SERVICE DURING 2013

• LEE HOWARD

BAE Systems HAWK T 1

Engine 1 x Adour Mk 151 5200 lbs thrust.
Crew 1 or 2 Pilots

Notes
Used by the Fleet Requirements and Aircraft Direction Unit (FRADU) at RNAS Culdrose to provide support for RN and foreign ships working-up with FOST; with the RN Flying Standards Flight and as airborne targets for the Aircraft Direction School. The aircraft are operated by Babcock and have civilian pilots and maintainers.

• LEE HOWARD

Eurocopter AS365N DAUPHIN 2

Engines 2 x Turbomeca Arriel 1C1.
Crew 1 or 2 pilots.

Operated under a Civil-Owned Military Registered, COMR, contract; 2 of these helicopters are used to support FOST staff with personnel transfers to ships in the Plymouth areas and a number of other tasks including system calibration and training operators for the control of naval gunfire support. They are based at Newquay Airport and use HMS RALEIGH at Torpoint as a 'lily pad' for picking up and dropping off passengers during the week.

© CROWN COPYRIGHT/MoD 2011

Beech AVENGER T1

Engines 2 x Pratt & Whitney PT 6A turboprops.
Crew 1 or 2 pilots; up to 4 student observers plus instructors.

Notes

Four aircraft developed from the King Air 350 ER have operated with 750 NAS since October 2011 in the observer training role. They are used for the third phase of training at RNAS Culdrose; the first two phases are flown in the Grob Tutors of 703 NAS at RAF Barkston Heath.

LEE HOWARD

GROB TUTOR T1

Engine 1 x Lycoming 0 - 360 - A1B6 piston engine
Crew 1 or 2 pilots

Notes
Used by 703 NAS at RAF Barkston Heath for the elementary training of RN pilots and observers and by 727 NAS at RNAS Yeovilton for the flying grading of new entry aircrew and other light, fixed-wing tasks.

ADRIAN PINGSTONE

Eurocopter SQUIRREL HT1

Engine 1 x Turbomeca Ariel 1D1
Crew 1 or 2 pilots and up to 4 passengers

Notes
Used by 705 NAS, part of the Defence Helicopter Flying School at RAF Shawbury, to provide basic helicopter flying training for pilots before they move on to fly operational types at RN Air Stations.

Royal Navy Historic Flight

The Royal Navy Historic Flight, based at RNAS Yeovilton, consists of several historic air-craft kept on the military register, maintained by civilians under a MoD contract and flown by the unit's commanding officer assisted by volunteer naval pilots in the display season. The present collection includes Swordfish I W 5856, Swordfish II LS 326, Sea Fury FB 11 VR 930, Sea Fury T 20 VX 281, Sea Hawk WV 908 and Chipmunk T 10 WK 608. They are not usually all serviceable at the same time. Swordfish III NF 389 continues to undergo long-term restoration by BAE Systems at Brough.

Galileo MIRACH 100/5

792 NAS, the Fleet Target Group, based at RNAS Culdrose uses a small number of these unmanned target aircraft. If not destroyed, they descend into the sea by para-chute at the end of a sortie and can be refurbished for further use.

WEAPONS OF THE ROYAL NAVY

Sea Launched Missiles

Trident II D5

The American built Lockheed Martin Trident 2 (D5) submarine launched strategic missiles are Britain's only nuclear weapons and form the UK contribution to the NATO strategic deterrent. 16 missiles, each capable of carrying up to 6 UK manufactured thermonuclear warheads (but currently limited to 4 under current government policy), can be carried aboard each of the Vanguard class SSBNs. Trident has a maximum range of 12,000 km and is powered by a three stage rocket motor. Launch weight is 60 tonnes, overall length and width are 13.4 metres and 2.1 metres respectively.

Tomahawk (BGM-109)

This is a land attack cruise missile with a range of 1600 km and can be launched from a variety of platforms including surface ships and submarines. Some 65 of the latter version were purchased from America to arm Trafalgar class SSNs with the first being delivered to the Royal Navy for trials during 1998. Tomahawk is fired in a disposal container from the submarine's conventional torpedo tubes and is then accelerated to its subsonic cruising speed by a booster rocket motor before a lightweight F-107 turbojet takes over for the cruise. Its extremely accurate guidance system means that small targets can be hit with precision at maximum range, as was dramatically illustrated in the Gulf War and Afghanistan. Total weight of the submarine version, including its launch capsule is 1816 kg, it carries a 450 kg warhead, length is 6.4 metres and wingspan (fully extended) 2.54 m. Fitted in Astute & T class submarines.

Harpoon

The Harpoon is a sophisticated anti-ship missile using a combination of inertial guidance and active radar homing to attack targets out to a range of 130 km, cruising at Mach 0.9 and carrying a 227 kg warhead. Fitted to Type 23 frigates. It is powered by a lightweight turbojet but is accelerated at launch by a booster rocket.

Sea Viper (Aster 15/30)

Two versions of the Aster missile will equip the Type 45 Destroyer, the shorter range Aster 15 and the longer range Aster 30. The missiles form the weapon component of the Principal Anti Air Missile System (PAAMS). Housed in a 48 cell Sylver Vertical Launch system, the missile mix can be loaded to match the ships requirement. Aster 15 has a range of 30 km while Aster 30 can achieve 100 km. The prime external difference between the two is the size of the booster rocket attached to the bottom of the missile. PAAMS is to be known as Sea Viper in RN service.

Sea Dart

A medium range area defence anti aircraft missile powered by a ramjet and solid fuel booster rocket. Maximum effective range is in the order of 80 km and the missile accelerates to a speed of Mach 3.5. It forms the main armament of the Type 42 destroyer EDINBURGH. Missile weight 550 kg, length 4.4 m, wingspan 0.91 m.

Sea Wolf

Short range rapid reaction anti-missile missile and anti-aircraft weapon. The complete weapon system, including radars and fire control computers, is entirely automatic in operation. Type 23 frigates carry 32 Vertical Launch Seawolf (VLS) in a silo on the foredeck. Basic missile data: weight 82 kg, length 1.9 m, wingspan 56 cm, range c.5-6 km, warhead 13.4 kg. The VLS missile is basically similar but has jettisonable tandem boost rocket motors.

Air Launched Missiles

Sea Skua

A small anti-ship missile developed by British Aerospace arming the Lynx helicopters carried by various frigates and destroyers. The missile weighs 147 kg, has a length of 2.85 m and a span of 62 cm. Powered by solid fuel booster and sustainer rocket motors, it has a range of over 15 km at high subsonic speed. Sea Skua is particularly effective against patrol vessels and fast attack craft, as was demonstrated in both the Falklands and Gulf Wars.

Guns

114mm Vickers Mk8

The Royal Navy's standard medium calibre general purpose gun which arms the later Type 22s, Type 23 frigates and Type 42 destroyers. A new electrically operated version, the Mod 1, recognised by its angular turret, was introduced in 2001 and will be fitted in the Type 23, Type 42 and Type 45 classes. Rate of fire: 25 rounds/min. Range: 22,000 m. Weight of Shell: 21 kg.

Goalkeeper

A highly effective automatic Close in Weapons System (CIWS) designed to shoot down missiles and aircraft which have evaded the outer layers of a ships defences. The complete system, designed and built in Holland, is on an autonomous mounting and includes radars, fire control computers and a 7-barrel 30 mm Gatling gun firing 4200 rounds/min. Goalkeeper is designed to engage targets between 350 and 1500 metres away.

Phalanx

A US built CIWS designed around the Vulcan 20 mm rotary cannon. Rate of fire is 3000 rounds/min and effective range is c.1500 m. Fitted in Destroyers, OCEAN, Wave, Bay and Fort Victoria classes. Block 1B began entering service from 2009. Incorporates side mounted Forward looking infra-red enabling CIWS to engage low aircraft and surface craft. In October 2012 it was announced that a further five Phalanx `Block 1B mountings were to be procured to protect RFA ships

DS30B 30mm

Single 30mm mounting carrying an Oerlikon 30mm gun. Fitted to Type 23 frigates and various patrol vessels and MCMVs. In August 2005 it was announced that the DS30B fitted in Type 23 frigates was to be upgraded to DS30M Mk 2 to include new direct-drive digital servos and the replacement of the earlier Oerlikon KCB cannon with the ATK Mk 44 Bushmaster II 30 mm gun. Consideration is already being given to purchasing additional DS30M Mk 2 systems for minor war vessels and auxiliaries.

GAM BO 20mm

A simple hand operated mounting carrying a single Oerlikon KAA 200 automatic cannon firing 1000 rounds/min. Maximum range is 2000 m. Carried by most of the fleet's major warships except the Type 23 frigates.

20mm Mk.7A

The design of this simple but reliable weapon dates back to World War II but it still provides a useful increase in firepower, particularly for auxiliary vessels and RFAs. Rate of fire 500-800 rounds/min.

Close Range Weapons

In addition to the major weapons systems, all RN ships carry a variety of smaller calibre weapons to provide protection against emerging terrorist threats in port and on the high seas such as small fast suicide craft. In addition it is sometimes preferable, during policing or stop and search operations to have a smaller calibre weapon available. Depending upon the operational environment ships may be seen armed with varying numbers of pedestal mounted General Purpose Machine Guns (GPMG). Another addition to the close in weapons is the Mk 44 Mini Gun a total of 150 of which have been procured from the United States as a fleetwide fit. Fitted to a naval post mount, the Minigun is able to fire up to 3,000 rounds per minute, and is fully self-contained (operating off battery power).

Torpedoes

Stingray

A lightweight anti submarine torpedo which can be launched from ships, helicopters or aircraft. In effect it is an undersea guided missile with a range of 11 km at 45 knots or 7.5 km at 60 knots. Length 2.1 m, diameter 330 mm. Type 23s have the Magazine Torpedo Launch System (MTLS) with internal launch tubes. Sting Ray Mod 1 is intended to prosecute the same threats as the original Sting Ray but with an enhanced capability against small conventionally powered submarines and an improved shallow-water performance.

Spearfish

Spearfish is a submarine-launched heavyweight torpedo which has replaced Tigerfish. Claimed by the manufacturers to be the world's fastest torpedo, capable of over 70 kts, its sophisticated guidance system includes an onboard acoustic processing suite and tactical computer backed up by a command and control wire link to the parent submarine. Over 20ft in length and weighing nearly two tons, Spearfish is fired from the standard 21-inch submarine torpedo tube and utilises an advanced bi-propellant gas turbine engine for higher performance.

Future Weapons

Future Anti-Surface Guided Weapon (Heavy)

This project, led by MBDA (UK) and derived from the company's existing 15km range Sea Skua Anti-Ship Missile, will provide the lead in to a 100kg weapon family that will include the Selected Precision Effects at Range (SPEAR) air-launched weapon for the Royal Air Force. Using an Imaging Infra Red (IIR) seeker capability, the project will be developed in collaboration with France, which has a similar anti-ship missile requirement, the Anti Navire Léger. It will provide the main armament for the RN's AW159 Lynx Wildcat and the French Navy's NH90 and Panther helicopters.

Future Anti-Surface Guided Weapon (Light)

Led by Thales (UK), this project will be based on the company's 6-8km range Lightweight Multi-role Missile (LMM). Weighing just 13kg it is designed to be fired from multiple ground, air and naval platforms against an equally wide range of targets up to, but not including Main Battle Tanks (MBTs). The RN variant is being developed to operate from the AW159 Lynx Wildcat helicopter.

Sea Ceptor (formerly known as FLAADS-M)

Incorporating the Common Anti-Air Modular Missile (CAAMM) family, being developed to replace the Rapier and Seawolf SAM systems, plus the ASRAAM short range Air-to-Air Missile. It will arm the Royal Navy's Type 23 frigates and its Type 26 Global Combat Ships. In Spring 2012 the MoD awarded MBDA UK a five-year Demonstration Phase contract worth £483 million to develop the missile for the RN.

At the end of the line ...

Readers may well find other warships afloat which are not mentioned in this book. The majority have fulfilled a long and useful life and are now relegated to non-seagoing duties. The following list gives details of their current duties:

Pennant No	Ship	Remarks
	BRITANNIA	Ex Royal Yacht at Leith. Open to the public.
	CAROLINE	Light Cruiser and veteran of the Battle of Jutland. Is to be restored and opened in 2014 as a tourist attraction at Belfast.
M29	BRECON	Hunt Class Minehunter - Attached to the New Entry Training Establishment, HMS RALEIGH, Torpoint, as a static Seamanship Training ship.
M103	CROMER	Single Role Minehunter - Attached to Britannia Royal Naval College, Dartmouth as a Static Training Ship.
L3505	SIR TRISTRAM	Refitted as a Static Range Vessel at Portland.
C35	BELFAST	World War II Cruiser Museum ship - Pool of London. Open to the public daily. Tel: 020 7940 6300
D23	BRISTOL	Type 82 Destroyer - Sea Cadet Training Ship at Portsmouth.
D73 S17	CAVALIER OCELOT	World War II Destroyer & Oberon class Submarine Museum Ships at Chatham. Open to the public. Tel: 01634 823800
F126 M1115	PLYMOUTH BRONINGTON	The ships remain at Birkenhead whilst discussions over their future continue.
S21	ONYX	At Barrow awaiting a new future as a proposed Submarine Heritage Centre will not now be opened.
S67	ALLIANCE	Submarine - Museum Ship at Gosport Open to the public daily. Tel: 023 92 511349
S50	COURAGEOUS	Nuclear-powered Submarine - On display at Devonport Naval Base. Can be visited during Base Tours. Tel: 01752 552326 for details.

Pennant No	Ship	Remarks
M1151	IVESTON	Static Sea Cadet Training Vessel (Thurrock)

At the time of publishing (December 2012) the following ships were laid up in long term storage or awaiting sale.

TREVOR GAUTREY

Stripped of anything useful, the Type 22 frigates CHATHAM, CORNWALL, CUMBERLAND and CAMPBELTOWN (left), together with the Type 42 destroyers LIVERPOOL (right) and MANCHESTER (centre), are seen laid up in Fareham Creek, Portsmouth, on 17 November 2012, awaiting disposal.

PORTSMOUTH: Ark Royal; Gloucester; Manchester; York; Liverpool; Chatham; Cornwall; Campbeltown; Cumberland; Walney.

PLYMOUTH: Trafalgar; Turbulent; Sceptre; Superb; Splendid; Spartan; Sovereign; Conqueror; Valiant; Warspite.

ROSYTH: Resolution; Renown; Repulse; Revenge; Swiftsure; Churchill; Dreadnought.

LIVERPOOL: Fort George.

Since the previous edition the following vessels in long term storage or awaiting scrap were disposed of:

BAYLEAF: Departed Portsmouth under tow tug CHRISTOS XXIII on 2 August 2012 bound for recycling at Leyal Shipbreakers, Turkey.